8 Unbreakable Rules For Business Start-Up Success

By Sean C. Castrina

8 Unbreakable Rules for Business Start-Up Success
By Sean C. Castrina
Copyright © 2013 Sean C. Castrina

ISBN-10: 0989104567
ISBN-13: 9780989104562
Library of Congress Control Number: 2013902028
Champion Publishing, Inc.
Charlottesville, Virginia

Champion
Publishing

PRAISE FOR 8 UNBREAKABLE RULES
FOR BUSINESS START-UP SUCCESS

"This remarkable book will save the aspiring entrepreneur 100's of hours and thousands of dollars on building a successful business. It can change your life."

–Brian Tracy,
Author of *The 100 Absolutely Unbreakable Laws of Business Success*
N.Y. Times Bestselling author and International Speaker

"*8 Unbreakable Rules* captures the soul of business that has made our country great and reveals how uncompromising character, respectful relationships and a commitment to the greater good of community lead to "uncommon" success and a life worth living."

-Dan Miller
N.Y. Times Bestselling Author of 48 Days to The Work You Love

"A thoughtful powerful book full of important advice for everyone thinking about starting a business."

-Edward D. Hess,
Professor of Business Administration & Batten Executive-in-Residence, Darden Graduate School of Business, Author of "Grow To Greatness."

"Starting a business is like finding your way around a dark room. This book is your flashlight; it provides practical and insightful guidance to find your way without hitting your hip on the corner of the table."

–Jerry Nemorin,
Founder and CEO of LendStreet

"I loves its simple language, written in a way that makes you want to keep reading and finally someone gives the real warning signs before you leap."

-Kirk Litton
Owner and President of Hometown Columbia Media
WWNU-FM & WWNX-FM   Columbia, SC

"In hindsight, I would say that **The 8 Unbreakable Rules** all applied to the successful building of my hedge fund. I would encourage any stock broker, fund manager, realtor or insurance broker to follow these 8 Rules in their efforts to build a successful business."

-Richard Kreitler
Founder Dakota Partners

"This book is real. I commend Sean on distilling the lessons he has learned the hard way into rules even entrepreneurs would not want to break."

-Saras D. Sarasvathy
University of Virginia, The Darden School
Author of "Effectuation"

"As I read through this compendium of excellent advice, I could only regret that it had not been written 40 years earlier; at a time when I really needed it. Even now, as a well seasoned entrepreneur, I will keep this book in my reference library."

-Ben Foster
President of Hightech Signs-Virginia

"This book provides insights into the process of planning and launching a business that demonstrate the author's seasoned perspective. This work will be a great benefit to anyone who is considering entrepreneurship."

-Robert Klonoski, JD, DMgt
Assistant Professor of Business Administration- Mary Baldwin College

"This book delivers straight talk to "the rest of us", the business wanabees who just need some no nonsense guidance to jump start the process of getting a business from no/where to now/here. A must read, and reread, for those who want to walk their talk and realize their dreams".

Peter van der Linde
Owner of van der Linde Reycling

"Obviously no book can guarantee success in your business journey but the principles in **"8 Unbreakable Rules"** sure can help you to avoid "unnecessary" catastrophes and stress."

-Matt Henderson
President and C.E.O. of MEMCO

"Our business depends on successfully recruiting entrepreneurs and providing them everything we can to help them succeed in their publishing business and this book will be a training manual."

-Carmen Ames
President of 'HomeTown" Magazines, Inc.

"Finally, a start-up book that tells you what the hell not to do."

-Mark Gordon
Owner of The Bike Factory

More endorsements can be found at www.8unbreakablerules.com

TABLE OF CONTENTS

ACKNOWLEDGEMENTS   xi
INTRODUCTION   xiii

RULE 1: YOU MUST BE QUALIFIED   **1**
It's Not Just About The Money   3
Understand The Risk   5
Entrepreneurs Think Differently   7
Can You Make Profitability Your Passion?   9
Are You A Self-Starter?   11
How Strong Is Your Success Instinct?   13
You Don't Need An Advanced Degree   15
Strong Work Ethic   17
Are You A Problem Solver?   19
Are You An Effective Time And Priority Manager?   21
Are You An Industry "Expert?"   23
Great People Skills Can Make The Difference   25
You May Be A Team Of One   27
Excel At The Right Business   29
Define Your Own Success Standard   31
Characteristics Of A High Risk Of Failure   33
"Never Give Up"   35

RULE 2: YOUR BUSINESS IDEA MUST BE QUALIFIED   **37**
Conduct Basic Market Research   39
Keep Your Business Model Simple   41
Fill A Need Or Meet A Desire   43
Focus On Durable Goods And Services   45
Unique Selling Proposition   47
Model A Franchise   49

Consider A Franchise   51
Start A Business - Or Purchase One   53
Buy The Company You Work For   55
Review Your Idea Thoroughly   57
Don't Quit Your Day Job   59

RULE 3: PLAN FOR SUCCESS   **61**
Obtain Competitive Intelligence   63
Obtain Baseline Pricing   65
Define Your Competitive Advantage   67
Mission Statement   69
Vision Statement   71
Value Statement   73
Financing Your Start-Up   75
Don't Count On Venture Capital   77
Create A Business Plan   79
Make An Exhaustive List Of Pre-Launch Tasks   81
Consider The Best Launch Season   83
Adapt To Changing Circumstances   85

RULE 4: PROTECT YOURSELF AND YOUR BUSINESS   **87**
Incorporate Your Business   89
Purchase Insurance   91
Protect Your Intellectual Property   93
If You Partner, Consider These Rules   95
Establish The Proper Legal Framework   97
Know All Applicable Labor Laws   99

RULE 5: BUILD A SUCCESSFUL TEAM   **101**
Qualify Your Labor Market   103
Try To Hire The Best, Regardless   105

There Are Mechanics To Hiring   107

Approach Staffing Strategically   109

If You Don't Have The Skills, Partner   111

Lead Like A Coach   113

Maximize The Talent Of Your Employees   115

Build And Trust Your "Cabinet"   117

Get To Know Your Local Bank   119

Develop A Support Group   121

RULE 6: MARKETING IS NOT OPTIONAL   **123**

Marketing Is More Than A Business Card   125

Marketing 101   127

Advertising 101   129

Who Is Your Ideal Customer?   131

What's In A Name? A Lot.   133

Elevator Pitch   135

Develop An Image   137

Yes, You Need A Website   139

Establish Your Reputation   141

Join Business Associations   143

Systematically Survey Customers   145

Develop Customer Testimonies   147

Look For Added Value   149

Start Branding Early   151

Promote "Word Of Mouth"   153

Develop A Start-Up Story   155

Your 1St Marketing Plan   157

Sales Process In Three Steps   159

RULE 7: KNOW YOUR NUMBERS   **161**

Know Your Operating Costs   163

Reserves 165
Credit Is Your Lifeblood 167
Take A Modest Salary 169
Avoid Unnecessary Expenses 171
Focus On Net Profit 173
Guard Your Accounts Receivable 175

RULE 8: LEARN FROM EXPERIENCE **177**
Don't Become Dependent 179
Handle Terminations With Care 181
The Customer Is Not Always Right 183
Dealing With Complaints 185
Trades 187
Jealously Guard Your Time 189
Start Over Every Year 191
Dream Big, Think Big 193
Keep A Start-Up Journal 195
Suggested Resources 199
Works Cited 203
Notes 211

States Patent Office. (n.d.). *Are You A Small Business?* Retrieved January 6, 2013, from USPTO.gov: http://www.uspto.gov/smallbusiness/

reet Journal. (n.d.). *How to Succeed as a Franchise.* Retrieved December 20, 2012, from WSJ.com: http://guides.wsj.com/small-business/franchising/how-to-succeed-as-a-franchisee/

amp, R., Levy, R., & Pruitt, B. (2012, March 19). *New Business Startups Declined in 2011, Annual Kauffman Study Shows.* Retrieved December 2, 2012, from Kauffman.org: http://www.kauffman.org/newsroom/new-business-startups-declined-in-2011-annual-kauffman-study-shows.aspx

(2012, October 29). *Online reputation.* Retrieved December 23, 2012, from USAToday.com: http://www.usatoday.com/story/money/business/2012/10/28/efficient-small-business-online-reviews/1654365/

, M. (2012, September 14). *10 Top Reasons Why First-Time Entrepreneurs Fail.* Retrieved November 24, 2012, from Entrepreneur.com: http://www.entrepreneur.com/article/223732

, M. (2011, January 28). *Four Ways to Keep Burn Rates Low.* Retrieved December 27, 2012, from BusinessInsider.com: http://www.businessinsider.com/high-burn-rates-result-in-short-startup-runways-2011-1

Portny, S. E. (2012, May). *Performing a Cost-Benefit Analysis.* Retrieved Dec
    25, 2012, from Dummies.com: http://www.dummies.com/how-to/co
    performing-a-costbenefit-analysis.html

Powell, C. (2012, June 4). *Battle Ready: Advice for startups from a seasoned v*
    Retrieved November 25, 2012, from Forbes.com: http://www.forbe
    forbes/2012/0604/entrepreneurs-advice-colin-powell-battle-ready.ht

Sellers, P. (2002, June 24). *Something To Prove Bob Nardelli was stunned*
    Jack Welch told him he'd never run GE. "I want an autopsy!" he dem
    Retrieved December 22, 2012, from Money.CNN.com: http://mon
    com/magazines/fortune/fortune_archive/2002/06/24/325190/index.

Spitznagel, E. (2012, April 26). *Rise of the Barter Economy.* Retrieved Dec
    26, 2012, from BusinessWeek.com: http://www.businesswee
    articles/2012-04-26/rise-of-the-barter-economy

Strauss, S. (2012, August 30). *Ask an Expert: Sure, be like Branson, bu*
    overdo it. Retrieved December 1, 2012, from USAToday.com:
    www.usatoday.com/story/money/columnist/strauss/2012/C
    strauss-small-business-risk-taking/1602125/

Symonds, M. (2009, March 19). *Diversifying Your Business.* Retrieved Decem
    2012, from IndustryWeek.com: http://www.industryweek.com/com
    amp-executives/diversifying-your-business

The Economist. (2009). *Brands and Branding.* (R. Clifton, Ed.) Canada: Bloo
    Press.

The Washington Post. (2012, March 22). *These are the customers you abs*
    must fire-right now. Retrieved December 25, 2012, from Washingto
    com: http://articles.washingtonpost.com/2012-03-22/business/354
    1_customers-clients-order-histories

Tracy, B. (2012, July 5). *Two Market Research Techniques for New B*
    Success. Retrieved December 1, 2012, from BrianTrac
    http://www.briantracy.com/blog/business-success/two-market-res
    techniques-for-new-business-success/

Dan (2012, June 25). Law of Attraction—Is it Magic? Retrieved February 1, 2013, from: http://www.48days.com/2012/06/25/law-of-attraction-is-it-magic/

L. H., & Robinson, D. (2010). *Driven: An Autobiography.* Salt Lake City, Utah: Deseret Book Co.

el, S. (2010, February 4). *Small Business Lending: How Big and Small Banks Compare.* Retrieved December 22, 2012, from ILSR.org: http://www.ilsr.org/charts-small-banks-small-business-lending/

ey, L. (n.d.). *The Disadvantages of Word of Mouth Advertising.* Retrieved January 6, 2013, from SmallBusiness.Chron.com: http://smallbusiness.chron.com/disadvantages-word-mouth-advertising-26133.html

al Business Research Institute. (n.d.). *Proactive Use of Customer Surveys Increases Profits.* Retrieved December 23, 2012, from NBRI.com: http://www.nbrii.com/customer-survey-white-papers/proactive-use-of-customer-surveys-increases-profits/

i, M. (2011, September 14). *Financial Advisors: 7 Steps for Replacing Distractions with Goals.* Retrieved December 31, 2012, from WealthManagement.com: http://wealthmanagement.com/practice-management/financial-advisors-7-steps-replacing-distractions-goals

The Small Business Network. (n.d.). *Line of Credit Basics.* Retrieved December 23, 2012, from NYTimes.com: http://www.nytimes.com/ref/open/finance/OPEN-CREDIT-BASICS.html

I, M. (2012, July 3). *Are you really adding value to your customers?* Retrieved December 23, 2012, from RecruitLoop.com: http://recruitloop.com/blog/are-you-really-adding-value-to-your-customers/

s, C. (2012, March 9). *Are You Raising Too Much Money?* Retrieved December 27, 2012, from Inc.com: http://www.inc.com/cindy-padnos/are-you-raising-too-much-money.html

I, S. (2012, July 4). *10 Tips for Being More Independent With Your Small Business.* Retrieved December 25, 2012, from SmallBizTrends.com: http://smallbiz-trends.com/2012/07/10-tips-being-independent-small-business.html

Jackson, E. (2011, December 14). *Top Ten Reasons Why VC-Backed Compani*
    Retrieved February 16, 2013, from Forbes.com: http://www.forbes.com
    ericjackson/2011/12/14/top-ten-reasons-why-vc-backed-companies-f

Jackson, N. M. (2012, June 25). *6 Steps to a Successful Business Launch.* Re
    November 24, 2012, from Entrepreneur.com: http://www.entrepreneu
    article/223732

James, G. (2012, April). *What is Success? Here's a Better Definition.* Re
    December 30, 2012, from INC.com: http://www.inc.com/geoffrey-
    what-is-success-better-definition.html

Khosla, V. (2012, July 13). *Maintain the Silicon Valley Vision.* Retrieved Dec
    2, 2012, from NYTimes.com: http://bits.blogs.nytimes.com/2012/
    khosla-the-silicon-valley-vision/

Kurtis, R. (2007, June 6). *Dealing with Customer Complaints.* Retrieved Decem
    2012, from School-for-Champions.com: http://www.school-for-cham
    com/tqm/complaints.htm

Lee, B. (1998). *The Power Principle: Influence with Honor.* New York, NY: Firesi

Lesonsky, R. (2012, February 21). *Are You Hiring Your Clone?* Retrieved Dec
    22, 2012, from SmallBizDaily.com: http://www.smallbizdaily.com
    are-you-hiring-your-clone/

Lloyd, M. (n.d.). *Why Smart Managers Hire Experience.* Retrieved December 22
    from WorkForce50.com: http://www.workforce50.com/Content/A
    ML2-Smart-Managers-Hire-Experience.cfm

Logue, A. C. (2012, June). Beyond the Handshake. *Entrepreneur*, p. 92.

Marcella, D. (n.d.). *Develop a Strategic Marketing Plan.* Retrieved Decemb
    2012, from StartupNation.com: http://www.startupnation.com/bu
    articles/1263/1/strategic-marketing-plan.asp

McLoone, S. (2009, August 10). *Small Business: Are Association Membe*
    Worth It? Retrieved December 23, 2012, from MainSree
    http://www.mainstreet.com/article/small-business/small-bus
    are-association-memberships-worth-it?page=1

nX. (2012, November 11). *Top Five Characteristics of Great Company Logos.* Retrieved December 18, 2012, from DivisionX.com: www.divisionx.com/articles/top-five-characteristics-of-great-company-logos/

ds, G. (2012, October 30). *Entrepreneurial Tightropes: Set your own pace.* Retrieved December 1, 2012, from USAToday.com: http://www.usatoday.com/story/money/columnist/edmunds/2012/10/30/gladys-edmunds-growth-pace/1669337/

reneur. (n.d.). *How to Name Your Business.* Retrieved December 22, 2012, from Entrepreneur.com: www.entrepreneur.com/article/21774

r, W. (n.d.). *Thoughts on the Business of Life.* Retrieved December 23, 2012, from Forbes.com: http://thoughts.forbes.com/thoughts/salesmanship-william-feather-once-you-have

J. A. (2000, November 1). *Collection: Days Saved, Thousands Earned.* Retrieved December 25, 2012, from Inc.com: http://www.inc.com/magazine/19951101/2488.html

J. (2012, June 29). *How Much Should You Pay Yourself?* Retrieved December 23, 2012, from NYTimes.com: http://boss.blogs.nytimes.com/2010/06/29/how-much-should-you-pay-yourself/

, R. (2011, May 4). *8 Insurance Coverages Every Entrepreneur Must Consider.* Retrieved December 10, 2012, from Under20CEO.com: http://under20ceo.com/8-insurance-coverages-every-entrepreneur-must-consider/

K. (n.d.). *7 Creative Ways to Get Customer Reviews.* Retrieved December 23, 2012, from Blog.Kissmetrics.Com: http://blog.kissmetrics.com/customer-testimonials/

s, C. (2012, December 8). *4 tips for small business hiring.* Retrieved December 4, 2012, from WashingtonPost.com: http://www.washingtonpost.com/business/4-tips-for-small-business-hiring/2011/12/08/gIQAMIgcsO_story.html

, M. (2012, March 3). *14 More Sales Motivation Quotes to Keep You Going!* Retrieved December 23, 2012, from TheSalesHunter.com: http://thesales-hunter.com/14-more-sales-motivation-quotes-to-keep-you-going/

ACKNOWLEDGEMENTS

I would like to thank first and foremost, my wife Bev, who has supported my own entrepreneurial journey and has allowed me to act on any idea no matter how crazy they first sounded. You, Mom, have been my biggest fan. To Baylee and Collin who have been so patient while I have been consumed with the writing of this book. And finally, to a new friend, author and professor Ed Hess, who I met this past year, and just happens to be one of finest business writers I have had the privilege of reading, even before our chance meeting. You have taken a personal interest in me, and this project, and I can only say thank you as each note and comment you made improved the book exponentially. Knowing the value of partnering allowed me to have a great team member, Daniel Veraldi, who helped with research and the final touches.

INTRODUCTION

Forbes Magazine has just released its annual list of the "400 Wealthiest Americans." It's quite an impressive list. It takes a minimum of $1.1 billion in personal wealth to be included. Collectively, these 400 people have more than $1 trillion in total assets. But the most impressive thing about the list is that 70% of those on it created their own wealth. That's right. They started with nothing more than an idea that they took action on.

So why should you listen to me? The answer is simple: I have successfully done what you are attempting to do, more than fifteen times. In America, one out of every two start-up companies fails within five years. Mine almost never have, though they were small companies. My employee rolls have never exceeded 20 people. In some cases, I had a single employee, maybe two. In fact, companies with less than 20 employees make up 88% of all U.S. businesses. Small business is the lifeblood of America's private sector success. My companies have ranged from direct mail, home services, home building and property management to retail.

My path to business success wasn't a natural one. It certainly didn't start with business school. In fact, my path fits more closely with what author Dan Miller says about success, "Success is never an accident. It typically starts as imagination, becomes a dream, stimulates a goal, grows into a plan of action—which then inevitably meets opportunity."[1] Once I'd already built several thriving companies, I decided to go back and read every start-up book I could get my hands on. I was curious to see if, entirely by accident or coincidence, I had followed all of the recommended steps. In fact this book is my attempt at "reverse engineering" my success.

I was shocked. I might never have become an entrepreneur, had I used most of these books for guidance. For example, many of them insist that you develop a comprehensive "business plan" as a critical qualifying step for starting a new company. I will speak about business plans, but it's not the big technical exercise that "experts" make it out to be. It's more like a fun game of detective, followed by some strategic planning exercises, as if you're going to battle.

Here's what I've learned: The main qualification for business ownership isn't your level of education or IQ; it's your aptitude, temperament, and attitude. You don't need an advanced degree—or even a college diploma—to become a successful entrepreneur.

Look at my "posse" of poker buddies, the majority are self-made millionaires. The only one who is not, does not prioritize money as his goal. He craves freedom of schedule. Driving to work each day at lunchtime on his Harley is his definition of success, and who can argue? Only a few made it past high school. Across the table, a good friend who was introduced to roofing as a teenager now commands the field, and has a multimillion-dollar company reflecting his expertise.

Two others own specialty retail outlets in an area filled with super stores. With all the online shopping these days, they probably should be out of business. Instead, they continue to grow their profit.

Another visitor to our game owns the area's most popular restaurant, when so many other food establishments nearby have gone belly up.

What sets us apart? We all started with what we believed was a good idea and decided to take action on it. We navigated the market using our instincts and our grasp of some intuitive fundamentals. And we took risks, but not reckless risks. Nowadays, we sit around and plan trips to events like the Daytona 500 or the Super Bowl. We spend days in these locales living it up with our families, while our businesses continue to bring in the sales.

This book is intended to share with you the wealth of entrepreneurial experience I have acquired over many years of building successful companies, most of which started as little more than an idea and none with more than $10,000 of initial start-up capital.

ORGANIZATION OF THE BOOK

The book is organized around 8 chapters that present what I call **8 UNBREAKABLE RULES for Business Start-Up Success**. I have boiled the book down to these rules for a reason. **They work**. In fact, I am confident that following these rules will increase the likelihood of start-up success. They offer guidance on how to establish, build, and grow a business, so they should be observed scrupulously.

Within each of my 8 UNBREAKABLE RULES, I present a series of LESSONS. These are backed by the practical experience of successful business owners like me, including business case studies and anecdotes that illustrate the lessons.

At the end of each lesson, I list two diagnostic questions. I then summarize the lesson's key takeaway. I close with a recommended concrete action step.

Chapter 1, **You Must Be Qualified**, helps you identify whether you are ready to be a business owner. Do you have the necessary skills and personality traits to succeed?

In Chapter 2, **Your Business Idea Must Be Qualified,** I provide lessons to help you identify and inventory whether your business idea is likely to be a winner. Plenty of good ideas never actually fly because there isn't a market for them—at least not a profitable one.

Chapter 3, **Plan for Success**, offers you practical business planning advice to put you on the path to success.

In Chapter 4, **Protect Yourself and Your Business**, you'll gain insight into the many ways you can protect yourself and your business in advance of opening your doors. Many businesses actually skip this step and end up paying dearly for it later.

The next step is Chapter 5, **Build a Successful Team**, if you have business partners or co-owners, you may have started on this step early on. Identifying the right people to work for you, and with you, can make or break a business.

After these 5 steps are in place, you'll need Chapter 6: **Marketing is Not Optional**, to attract your customers. Many businesses fail because they have not accepted how fundamental marketing is to their success.

In Chapter 7, **Know Your Numbers**, I teach you to think critically about your operating costs, pricing structure, and how much income you will need to meet your own personal expenses. Even if you don't love math, being successful with your start-up requires that you know your basic business arithmetic.

The last rule, Chapter 8, is **Learn from Others**. Here I share lessons from both successes and failures. I also offer you some special gems from myself, and my "poker buddies," things we've learned as we've built our companies—and made millions.

Introduction

After digesting the 8 rules and nearly 100 concise practical lessons presented in this book, you'll have the vital tools you need to increase your chances of building a profitable start-up company. I encourage you to return to these lessons more than once and to participate thoughtfully in the suggested exercises. Good luck on your start-up business adventure!

[*1*]

YOU MUST BE QUALIFIED

The first rule of successful business is that you—the business owner—must be qualified to start and operate a business. You may have picked up this book because you've always dreamed of owning your own business, but you're not really sure you have what it takes. The lessons in this section will help you learn about all the skills, personality traits, and habits that should help you be a successful business owner. They will also show you the harsh reality of starting up a business. If it's not what you expected, I'm happy to have saved you the time, money, and heartache by learning these lessons now.

IT'S NOT JUST ABOUT THE MONEY

Before you take the leap and start a business, ask yourself, "Why am I starting this business in the first place?" Does this reason excite you? This reason needs to be more than money, as this will probably be the last reward for your hard work. Yes, you want to start and own a profitable business but you need to have reasons other then money to motivate you in those challenging times.

There are many reasons why you might want to start a business. The most obvious one—according to nearly every survey—is the desire to make more money. That translates into improving your standard of living. The second most popular reason is greater flexibility and independence, meaning the opportunity to have more control over your future. Gladys Edmunds of USA Today writes, "The primary purpose of having your own business is so that it can become the catalyst to affording you a life worth living." [2]

However, there are usually deeper reasons for owning your own business. A passion to innovate. A need to challenge yourself to achieve things that others would find difficult—and may not dare attempt. A desire to put your own unique stamp on the world. The determination to build a great team. A willingness to "serve" others.

In fact, to be totally motivated by the idea of making money rarely breeds success. If it did, a lot more start-ups would succeed. Think of the great entrepreneurs of recent times. Steve Jobs had plenty of opportunities to cash out and live a life of ease, after launching Apple. But he was constantly driven to make better products and dominate more of the market for computers, leading him to work up until his death at building an even stronger company.

Ask yourself why you are going into business in the first place. Does the answer truly excite you? Remembering your deepest motivations is likely to sustain you in your business over the long haul, especially during difficult times, when you could be tempted to turn back.

TAKEAWAY:

Motivations other than money will help you stay committed to your business, day in, day out.

THOUGHTS TO CONSIDER:

1. Why do you want to go into business?
2. Will this reason still excite and motivate you a year from now?

ACTION STEP:

Write down the reasons for starting your business and keep it in your wallet, or somewhere close, so you can view it often.

UNDERSTAND THE RISK

It is a common misconception that to start a business and succeed you must take big risks. The truth is that smart entrepreneurs take well-thought-out risks. Lawyer, Steve Strauss warns against unnecessary risk: "...risk is part of the game. It is the juice. The problem is, because entrepreneurs have that gambler's mentality, they can, at times, underestimate the risk involved. Or maybe they know the risk, but like it anyway."[3] A well-thought-out risk means being prepared if things don't go your way.

It is a rare situation that you "bet the ranch" on your business idea. The only time you can bend this rule is if you are in your twenties or thirties so that you may have time to re-coup your losses if your business idea doesn't work out.

In his late 50s, my dad received a disability settlement and thought it would be a great idea to own a bar. Of course, it failed for all the reasons businesses fail. The worst part was that he was not at an age where he could ever earn his money back. To this day, he laments what this failure has cost him in regards to his current standard of living. It was a risk he could ill afford to make at the time he did.

Be careful how much you put at risk in regard to personal capital. If your business fails, would you lose your home or kid's college fund? If the answer is "yes" then in my opinion, the potential for loss is too great to move forward. I would also strongly encourage you to communicate to those whose lives failure could affect that you have not "bet the ranch" and that you have carefully thought out the risks. I have been fortunate to have an amazing wife who has supported me on my business ventures, but I have also always communicated to her, in detail, what I was investing, prior to moving forward.

TAKEAWAY:
You do not have to take a great risk to be a success.

THOUGHTS TO CONSIDER:
1. If your business failed would you lose your home or children's college fund?
2. How much personal capital can you afford to invest into your business without taking a great risk?

ACTION STEP:
Honestly answer the questions above. These may simply be the most important questions you ask.

ENTREPRENEURS THINK DIFFERENTLY

Entrepreneurism is my word of the day, but the problem is, I cannot find a definition of it. When I look it up, it says it is another word for entrepreneur. I don't think that is true, because I want a word for a person that studies entrepreneurs. Ok, maybe entrepreneurist is a word, but my computer spell check just highlighted this word informing me it is not a word. This is bothering me because who studies entrepreneurs? I think Saras D. Sarasvathy in her groundbreaking book *Effectuation: Elements of Entrepreneurial Expertise* is the first and only book I have read that says, and I am going to give it to you in my language, "Entrepreneurs are unique in how they think and process information." This is the most exhaustive look into what, and who an entrepreneur is. I will warn you, this is some tough reading in that the author provides countless studies written out in detail.

I have said all this to point out that entrepreneurs think differently from other people, and the book, *Effectuation,* lets me know I am not crazy in how I think. Remember Algebra 1 where A + B = C? Most people have to know what A and B are to know what C (desired result) is. Entrepreneurs start with C (an idea for a successful business that provides freedom/ money) and know *either* A or B—they rarely know both. The fact is you cannot know or control all the factors needed to guarantee a successful business. Your original business and its plan, which is important, will evolve though. As Scott Allison of Forbes Magazine put it, "You don't know what you don't know, and you don't know what the market wants, until you build something and show it to them."[4] Ten years from now you will laugh at what you and this original business are doing. It will morph, and I am just letting you know in advance, that that is great, because that is what makes us unique.

TAKEAWAY:
Entrepreneurs think differently.

THOUGHTS TO CONSIDER:
1. Do you need all the facts before moving forward on something?
2. Are you consumed with how things work or are you just glad they work? (Hint: I just want things to work, the how is not that important to me.)

ACTION TO TAKE:
Begin this start-up journey knowing you cannot plan for everything.

CAN YOU MAKE PROFITABILITY YOUR PASSION?

It is great if you can do what you love to do and get paid for it. However, in many cases your passion will not earn you a living. I wish someone would pay me to play golf, and tennis, but I have yet to meet this person. I establish businesses, in some cases, for no other reason than to make money. That is the motivation I need because having money allows me to do the things I am passionate about. I know early in this chapter I said money should not be your first and only motivation to start a business. What I am saying here is your passion is not always profitable.

Years ago I had trouble finding good contractors for a home improvement project. No one showed up on time, and the contract price kept changing. I saw, firsthand, that there was a need for this type of business. My thinking was that answering the phone with a friendly voice, providing a fair written estimate, showing up on time, and doing quality work would make a profitable business. It was not my passion, but that was beside the point. Within two months I launched Advantage Handyman Services, 3 divisions, numerous sister companies, and millions of dollars later, it has paid for a lot of golf and tennis, among other new passions that I can now afford to have.

If you are passionate about something that also seems like good business sense, you are one of the lucky ones who can go into a business that you have a passion for. In *Creating a Business You'll Love,* Tim Berry, founder of Palo Alto Software and bplans.com, explains, "There is nothing as important as offering value... The clichés say it's about doing what you love, being passionate, and sticking to it. I say yes, that is important, but you absolutely must temper that with making sure you're doing something that offers value to others. Maybe you love playing the guitar or painting with watercolors, but will people spend their money to hear you play?"[5] Of course, keep in mind that when you turn your passion into a business, it can turn fun into work. Sometimes it is best to pursue your passion purely as a passion and find some other way to pay for it.

TAKEAWAY:
You will not always be paid for your passion.

THOUGHTS TO CONSIDER:
1. Is your passion something someone will pay you to do?
2. Would additional income and schedule flexibility allow you to participate in your passion more?

ACTION STEP:
If your business is not your passion, find images or brochures that reflect your passion, and put them in a place where you will see them daily. This will be your motivation for your business. For example, if you love playing golf, maybe your motivation is a brochure of a nice country club that you would love to join.

ARE YOU A SELF-STARTER?

Starting a business requires the ability to make something from nothing. This is more important than just having an idea. The ability to initiate something, from nothing more than an idea, into a functioning organization, is what is required. Allow these words from noted motivational speaker and author, Tony Robbins, to shed light on initiative. "Success comes from taking initiative and following up...persisting. To produce a new momentum toward success in your life."

Did you ever have a lemonade stand? You decided you needed extra money, it was hot outside, and your mom had extra lemonade mix. So a half hour later; up went your creative sign to attract those driving by, as you enthusiastically served your product.

In short, you had all the needed components, so you took initiative and made something happen.

I have read more articles then I have fingers, on the qualities needed to succeed as an entrepreneur. And without exception, being a self-starter was consistently in the top 5 of each list.

Did you organize fraternity parties in college? As an adult, maybe you started a neighborhood watch or a fantasy football league? It is this initiative, the energy to take the first step, and organizational skills, that are required to get something going.

The entrepreneur must be a doer. Think back on a time in your life when you were a doer, and ask yourself whether you can be that person right now. If so, you might be able to start a business.

I have met many people that have good business ideas but zero initiative. "The most common cause of startup failure is the entrepreneur just gets tired, gives up, and shuts down the company," writes start-up mentor and blogger Martin Zwilling.[6] "Despite setbacks, many successful entrepreneurs, like Steve Jobs and Thomas Edison, kept slugging away on their vision until they found success." Starting a business requires personal dynamite. When you leave the area, everyone knows something happened.

TAKEAWAY:
You must be a self-starter.

THOUGHTS TO CONSIDER:
1. Think of at least three things you have initiated from nothing more than a desire, or an idea.
2. Do others follow you naturally?

ACTION STEP:
Make a list of times you have taken initiative to make something out of nothing. What have you succeeded at?

HOW STRONG IS YOUR SUCCESS INSTINCT?

An instinct is a natural impulse. Do you have the success instinct? In other words, do you expect to succeed in the things you do, or do you constantly harbor fears and doubts?

I start every day saying the following phrase to myself: "I expect to be successful today." This may seem silly, but psychology has proven that what we expect tends to become reality. In a column for the *Huffington Post,* William Zinke, chairman of the Spotlight on Entrepreneurship Summit, listed a "positive attitude" as one of the top three characteristics of successful entrepreneurs.

You must have a personal confidence that expects daily success. It is an inner wiring that naturally expects the best result in situations. This does not mean you are in fantasyland, only that you genuinely believe most coin tosses will go your way.

If you are a pessimist, and expect things to not go well, it is best to not start a business. I am being perfectly serious. In business, there are plenty of outside forces telling you that you are going to fail and that you should never have started a business. You don't need to lend your own voice to that chorus.

Pessimists tend to stop going the extra mile that it takes to be successful, as an entrepreneur. Optimists feel that their extra effort will be rewarded, and this becomes a self-fulfilling prophecy.

Start each day with a positive outlook, expecting the best outcome of each situation. This attitude is contagious and will permeate to your employees. This creates an exciting work atmosphere.

I like what author, Brian Tracy says, "Winners make a habit of manufacturing their own positive expectations in advance of the event."

TAKEAWAY:
An optimistic and or positive attitude is a characteristic of successful entrepreneurs.

THOUGHTS TO CONSIDER:
1. Are you a positive or negative person?
2. Can you tell when you are around a negative person? Does it drain you?

ACTION STEP:
Start each day with a positive attitude.

YOU DON'T NEED AN ADVANCED DEGREE

It is no surprise to learn that doctors earn the highest income in America. From surgeons to dentists and orthodontists, the average income for these professionals ranges from $160,000 to $260,000 per year.

However, consider all that is required to get into one of these occupations: the smarts, the long years of schooling, and the large student loans. I am happy to report that you can make the same income—or more—as a savvy businessman.

That's right. I started one of my first businesses with only a $10,000 initial investment. I made as much money as a surgeon typically does. In more recent years, I have earned far more.

On this year's Forbes 400 list of the wealthiest American's, 70% are entrepreneurs who had no quality in common other than having a powerful business idea and the initiative to pursue it. Anyone—absolutely anyone—can be wealthy as a successful business owner, if you have the basic aptitude and are willing to become the master of your own habits.

Perhaps you've clicked past job listings that required advanced degrees you don't have. That career ceiling typically disappears for successful entrepreneurs. In fact, college graduates experienced the largest slump in new business creation for 2011.[7] Unlike a human resources department, most of your customers aren't worried about what pieces of paper are hanging on the business owner's wall.

Let me put it this way: You really do have to be "qualified" to be an entrepreneur. You just don't have to be "credentialed."

TAKEAWAY:

You do not have to go through years of schooling or take on massive debt to be wealthy as a business owner.

THOUGHTS TO CONSIDER:

1. Do you feel limited by a lack of education?
2. Do you feel limited in your income potential?

ACTION STEP:

Put limited thinking behind you and know that you have no limits as an entrepreneur.

STRONG WORK ETHIC

I like what former Secretary of State, Colin Powell says about hard work as it relates to success, "A dream doesn't become reality through magic; it takes sweat, determination and hard work."

I very recently purchased a business and retained its previous owner. From day one I began to realize this person did not like mornings. It was impossible to speak with this individual before 9am. I purchased the business because it was struggling and it complimented one of my current businesses, and I decided to retain this previous owner because they had expertise that I desperately needed at the time. However, right from the start I could tell why this person struggled as a business owner. This person simply did not have the work ethic required to be successful.

Each business requires a different time commitment needed to be successful. Some will require early mornings, and some, like restaurants, will require late evenings. The specifics are not important, other than that you have a commitment to work hard and take the lead at those crucial times.

A family member of mine once purchased a restaurant and thought that he could come to work at 2pm and it would still succeed as long as he had key employees running the operation. Or so he thought. Instead, the business failed. He set the wrong example, and everyone—from employees to customers—took their lead from him.

In the beginning, as you're starting up your business, you have to commit to do whatever it takes in regards to time and work commitment to make the business succeed. It is essential to show your employees that you will do whatever it takes. Whenever possible—and that means regularly—be the first one in and the last one out.

Here's the encouraging equation that has always worked for me: I worked hard in the beginning and made very little money. After two to three years, I worked only a little and made a lot of money.

TAKEAWAY:

For your business to be a success it will require a strong work ethic.

THOUGHTS TO CONSIDER:

1. Are you a "morning person?" If not, is your drive to succeed a motivator to get you up early in the morning?
2. Can you work long days for as long as it may take to be successful?

ACTION STEP:

Prepare yourself for working long days initially, to make the business succeed. Tell your family of your plan and ask for their understanding of your commitment to the business.

ARE YOU A PROBLEM SOLVER?

I like to think that I am able to do my best thinking when things are the toughest. I have been in meeting with business owners who, when faced with a problem or options that have consequences, simply become paralyzed.

As a business owner, you must be able to solve problems, and in most cases, quickly. You must not be paralyzed by a crisis or impending decision. Just know, that based on the information you have at the time, you are making the best—and therefore, the "right" decision.

The fact is you're going to make decisions that, in hindsight, weren't correct. Larry Levy of the Kellogg School of Management confirms this value. Two of the three qualities he sees in successful entrepreneurs are the following:

- Learn from mistakes and don't repeat them.
- Be willing to live with occasional failure.

In other words, you will make mistakes. Don't wring your hands. Make the best decision that you can.

Experts on wilderness survival often say that it is better to make the wrong decision at the right time then to make no decision at all. When you stop making decisions, you're dead.

One additional piece of advice: Rarely do you have to solve the problem the second you hear of it. I sometimes get calls at 8am with a problem. I used to feel like I had to solve it on that phone call. I have learned to now say, "Let me get all the facts, and I will get back with you later today." It is amazing how one hour of thinking can improve your decisions.

Of course some critical decisions will need to be made on the spot, but they are few. I have also put together a series of questions, related to my businesses that I will run through before making a decision.

TAKEAWAY:
You cannot be paralyzed when facing a crisis or big decision.

THOUGHTS TO CONSIDER:
1. Do you need to gather a lot of information before making a decision?
2. Do you have trouble making decisions?

ACTION STEP:
Create a process that allows you to make decisions in a timely manner. It helps if you list a series of questions to run through when a decision has to be made.

ARE YOU AN EFFECTIVE TIME AND PRIORITY MANAGER?

Are you productive? Can you identify what needs to get done and actually do it? At the end of the day, have you accomplished profitable tasks? Being a workaholic will not guarantee success, but the ability to accomplish high priority tasks will.

The website Under30CEO.com says that being focused and disciplined enough to take steps every day towards achieving your objectives is the number one quality of successful entrepreneurs.[8] Wealth Management.com describes that same quality as the ability to know what you want and to resist activities that might distract you from pursuing your goals.[9]

There are very few skills more beneficial to master in business, than time and priority management. The ability to start each day knowing what must be done, and the discipline to do it, is a personality trait that the successful have mastered. Small business expert, Rhonda Abrams, warns her readers, "Identify the most important ingredients for your success and make sure you're concentrating on those. Don't let urgent but unimportant matters keep you from the really important stuff."[10]

If you have never read a book on time management, I would encourage you to add this to your "to do list." If you have read a book, or been to a seminar on time management but have not implemented these skills into your life, START NOW.

You also need to identify what tasks only you, as the business owner, can do. Others may handle product ordering and even staff hiring. In fact, "Many get to a point where it makes sense to consider outsourcing the most basic daily operational chores," according to USA Today's Bryan Acohido. "Then precious resources can be redirected to tasks directly related to growth, such as customer relations, production and sales."[11] In my business, however, only I can write the radio and TV commercials and all meetings with the accountant, though rarely fun, I must undertake.

There should be tasks that only you have the authority or the expertise to perform. Whether it's big things or small things, your job is to do the things nobody else can.

Learn not to confuse the elements of motion with progress. Progress always requires motion, but motion isn't always progress according to Larry H. Miller.[12] I recently heard golf analyst David Feherty say, "Successful people do what un-successful people do not want to do." That sums it up quite nicely!

TAKEAWAY:
Time and priority management are skills that effective people, and successful business owners, have mastered.

THOUGHTS TO CONSIDER:
1. Have you ever been to a time management seminar? Are there any available you can attend?
2. Do you feel like you are a good manager of your time?

ACTION STEP:
Read a book on time management or attend a seminar before your first day of business.

ARE YOU AN INDUSTRY "EXPERT?"

Will you know your industry better than anyone who works for you? Will you have an area within your industry that you will know better than anyone else? Seek to be an expert in something within your business. Customers and employees can tell when you have no idea what is going on. The good news is that they can also tell when you have a keen understanding of an area as well. You do not need to know everything within your business better than everyone, but there needs to be an area of knowledge that you are the authority on.

I recently learned that if you read two books on a specific subject, you would know more than 95% of everyone else. Continue to learn, whether from reading books, going to trade association conferences, or training seminars. Subscribe to industry magazines. Take whatever classes are needed to have all the respected licenses and certifications within your industry. To clarity, I am not saying degrees, but licenses and certifications that should take weeks or maybe months to receive.

I also encourage you to commit yourself to being a lifelong learner. Write and read blogs, and offer to teach a class at trade shows and local association meetings.

I have mentioned one of my earlier businesses, Advantage Handyman Services, where I began with no expertise so I partnered with someone who had the needed expertise. But within five years of starting this business I obtained the state's highest level licensing for our industry. I personally obtained this difficult license for two reasons. First, I did not want to be dependent on someone else who had my business hostage since I did not have this license requirement. Second, this high level license allowed us to move into new areas that tripled our income. I also gained credibility from my employees and counterparts for earning this license.

TAKEAWAY:
Be an expert in some area of your industry.

THOUGHTS TO CONSIDER:
1. Is there a license or certification that you do not have that would be valuable in your business?
2. When is the last time you read a book or took a class that related to the industry you are entering?

ACTION STEP:
Commit to reading a book, taking a class, or obtaining a license or certification in the next 90 days

GREAT PEOPLE SKILLS CAN MAKE THE DIFFERENCE

People do business with people they like and trust. This sounds simple, but I meet business owners all too often who have little or no people skills. They do not look you in the eye, or they interrupt when you are talking, just to name a few unwelcome characteristics. If you could only improve one thing about yourself that may have the greatest impact on your success, it would be having great people skills: the ability to have those who meet you, like you, and have confidence that you are trustworthy.

I look back on my direct mail magazine success and attribute it to my people skills more than any one thing. I had a direct mail magazine that featured a Domino's Pizza and McDonald's franchise. What made their advertising special was that the Domino's owner had been in litigation with the former magazine owner before me, and McDonalds did no local print advertising other then mine. (For the record, the magazine had failed and was not being printed when I started it). Later it was clear they advertised with me because they liked me personally. I quickly earned the trust of the Domino's franchisee with free advertising space to make amends for the previous owner, and persistent friendliness on the phone allowed me to break the ice of the McDonald's franchise owner. I would later play golf with both of these owners and it was my people skills that won their business.

People skills allow employees to want to work for you and be loyal. Your associates will want to network with you if you are likeable and trustworthy. And of course the customers you meet will trust your business if they trust you. If you aren't honest with people, business writers Michael Copeland and Om Malik warn, "They'll eventually learn the truth, and when they do, your credibility will be compromised. Permanently."[13]

If you could only read one book in the next year, I would encourage you to read Dale Carnegie's *How to Win Friends and Influence People*. It is simply the textbook on how to interact with others. Two others, if you wanted to develop this area, would be Stephen R. M. Covey's *The Speed of Trust* and John Maxwell's *25 Ways to Win with People*.

TAKEAWAY:

The ability to have people like you and trust you will benefit you more than any other skills you can obtain.

THOUGHTS TO CONSIDER:

1. Are you a good listener or do you interrupt people when they are talking?
2. Do you communicate with clarity and confidence?

ACTION STEP:

Commit to reading Dale Carnegie's *How to Win Friends and Influence People.*

YOU MAY BE A TEAM OF ONE

Owning your own business, especially during the first few start-up years, can be a lonely time. Some of you will have left your full-time employment to start your own company. Previously, your co-workers were people you've known and socialized with for years. Those days could well be over.

In a start-up business, you will have many people that I call "must hires." You hire them because you need them to perform certain tasks. There is no guarantee that you will ever have a personal relationship with them. You shouldn't expect to, in fact.

As a corollary, I would warn you to think long and hard before you hire a friend or family member to work in your business. Noam Wasserman, a Harvard Business School professor, says that business partnerships with friends and family are one of the most common decisions, "But that type of team is the least stable. It's the most likely to end up in disaster."[14] There is a great potential for misunderstanding, as the boundary lines and mutual expectations of your relationship start to change—as well they must.

I have a good friend who ended up having to fire his brother in-law. To say their last family reunion was awkward is an understatement. Letting a family member go— even more than a friend—can rebound in unpleasant ways.

There are reasons to hire people who are close to you. They can be loyal and trust-worthy partners and employees. However, hiring them contains inherent risks. As a rule, you might not want to depend on these relationships to operate your business.

I encourage you to find a social network such as sports league, church group, or poker night where you will have weekly interactions on a social level. Be prepared to look outside of your business for friendships. In general, family and friends, and business relationships should be kept separate.

Let the excitement and sense of fulfillment that is derived from being a successful business owner fill you to the brim as much as possible. Share those joys and challenges outside the workplace.

TAKEAWAY:
It can be very lonely in the beginning.

THOUGHTS TO CONSIDER:
1. Do you function well alone?
2. Identify a personality type that you enjoy being around, and seek to hire those who bring this.

ACTION STEP:
Prepare yourself for being alone a lot during your start-up years. Find social outlets outside of business. When you are ready to hire, try to hire someone you will enjoy being around.

EXCEL AT THE RIGHT BUSINESS

Success in one area does not always translate in another. I was meeting with my accountant, and we got in a discussion about why businesses fail. He told me about a successful accountant friend of his who had recently purchased a restaurant, and it was losing money. His friend said, "It was making money until I bought it. What am I doing wrong?" To which my accountant responded, "You're a great accountant. What led you to believe you could successfully own and operate a restaurant?" Or, for another well-known example: Do you remember when basketball legend Michael Jordan thought he would give professional baseball a try because he was good at it in high school? How did that turn out?

I am approached every few years about partnering in a restaurant. My response is always the same. NO. If you gave me a restaurant, I would give it back. Why? Because I have no idea how to run a restaurant. I mention restaurants because it seems that more start-ups are restaurants, and they have an extremely high failure rate. I think most people do not realize the amount of work required to own this type of business and the amount of daily cash flow required. Not only does it require a great deal of time, but you must also know the industry.

The hard truth is that your personal experience can only take your idea so far. Just because I am a successful business owner doesn't mean I can be successful at owning any type of business. Whether you think you know the industry or you already have a plan, you may have overestimated the demand or profitability for your good or service. We sometimes forget that billionaire Donald Trump once tried his hand at owning an airline.

TAKEAWAY:
Success in one career does not always translate to another.

THOUGHTS TO CONSIDER:
1. Do you believe your prior success can help you in this new business?
2. If so, why, and in what key areas?

ACTION STEP:
Talk to someone within the industry you are entering, and get a clear understanding of the time and talent required to succeed.

DEFINE YOUR OWN SUCCESS STANDARD

What would success look like to you personally? This is not the same as your vision statement that defines what success looks like for the company. Before you start this start-up journey, define success for you personally. It is hard to know when you have reached the finish line if you do not know where it is.

With a profitable career, ex-marketing exec Geoffrey James left marketing to pursue a new career. His advice is to understand that money isn't everything, but it helps. A profitable company is a way to achieve a happy life. James writes, "Being unhappy, of course, can definitely spur people to action. However, the action should be pointed at trying to become happier—not trying to become richer, in the rather naive belief that being rich, in and of itself, will make you happy."[15] What would be your "happy life"?

If you could have the perfect employment situation for yourself, what would it look like? How many hours would you work and how much money would you earn? Are there certain friends you would like to have working with you? Is there an impact you would like to make within your industry?

As you answer these questions on paper, this will become another document that I encourage you to refer back to regularly as you build your business. This will encourage you and keep you on course. Over time, your personal definition of success will evolve, but the initial one gets you started with a target.

TAKEAWAY:
Personal success needs to be defined prior to starting your business.

THOUGHTS TO CONSIDER:
1. How much money do you want to make? This figure should be a challenge, not a fairy tale.
2. How would you describe the perfect workweek? What hours will you work? What will you be doing, and who will you be working with?

ACTION STEP:
Write a clear definition of personal success in this business.

CHARACTERISTICS OF A HIGH RISK OF FAILURE

Why do half of all businesses fail? I am convinced it is not necessarily the business, but the person in charge. They have more than 1 or 2 weaknesses in key areas for personal success. I believe Napoleon Hill's classic "Think and Grow Rich" should be a high school class like arithmetic, spelling and grammar. I cannot think of one class that could be more valuable. I have personally studied at the undergraduate and graduate levels, though not in business, and have yet to learn more of how to succeed in life than what this book offers.

I want to give you a condensed, with slight modification, list of the characteristics of failure; what this book shares as to WHY people fail. After a 25-year study with over 25,000 interviews, the simple goal was to find out what qualities repeat themselves in successful people and what qualities repeat themselves in unsuccessful people. "Self-confidence is good," writes technology entrepreneur Eric Jackson. "But over-confidence is usually behind the most spectacular of failures."[16] So my advice is you would be wise to take a personal inventory and ask yourself prior to your journey, "Are there areas that I must improve if I plan to succeed?"

- Lack of clarity and focus
- Lack of ambition
- Lack of persistence
- Negativity
- Lack of knowledge
- Lack of spending control or poor money management
- Lack of enthusiasm
- Lack of flexibility
- Does not work well with others
- Lack of self-discipline
- Lack of leadership
- Dishonesty

- Lack of planning
- Indecision
- Lack of capital
- Ego

TAKEAWAY:
Identify weaknesses that are known to be the qualities of those who fail.

THOUGHTS TO CONSIDER:
1. From the list above, what characteristics of failure have the potential to limit your success?
2. What one change could you make that would have the most dramatic improvement of this weakness or these weaknesses?

ACTION STEP:
Commit to making the needed change or changes to overcome your identified area of weakness.

"NEVER GIVE UP"

One of the most moving speeches I have ever heard was by Jim Valvano, North Carolina State's legendary college basketball coach. Valvano, while suffering from late stage cancer, gave his "never give up" speech. If you have never heard it, I encourage you to seek it out on the Internet.

Nothing will bring you closer to giving up and calling it quits than starting a business. Prepare for some of the loneliest times in your life. There will be occasions when you will wonder what in the world you got yourself into. Just remember, rarely does something good come easy. I always thought to myself if it is tough for me, then it is tough for my competition. Maybe they will quit, but I know I will not.

In all the business books I have read, a common theme for success is fierce determination and perseverance. You need to be like a combat warrior whose mind is always prepared for battle and committed to survival. Take author Andy Andrews' advice to "persist without exception." His qualifier without exception is what separates successful people from unsuccessful.

I like this quote by gold medalist sprinter Jesse Owens: "We all have dreams. But in order to make dreams come into reality, it takes an awful lot of determination, dedication, self-discipline, and effort."

TAKEAWAY:
Success comes to those who are determined to persevere.

THOUGHT TO CONSIDER:
1. Do you have a history of quitting? Seriously, ask yourself and answer honestly!
2. Can you remember a time when you battled through something difficult?

ACTION STEP:
Know before you start that it will be difficult, so commit to persevere.

[2]

YOUR BUSINESS IDEA MUST BE QUALIFIED

This chapter provides lessons to help you assess whether your business concept is viable. Plenty of good ideas for products and services never fly because there simply isn't a market for them—at least not a profitable one. You need to be as tough and honest about the viability of your business idea as you are about your basic qualifications to be a business owner. Avoid wishful thinking. "If you build it, they will come?" Only if its foundation is sound— and you build it right.

CONDUCT BASIC MARKET RESEARCH

Just because you love golf and could use a driving range to improve your game, that doesn't mean a driving range is a good business idea. It shocks me how many businesses are started based purely on an individual's personal interests, and not good business sense.

In one shopping center where my office was located, there was a store selling model trains. A few doors down, there was another store selling NASCAR memorabilia. When you entered these stores and talked to the owners, you could tell this was their passion.

I would always see the same people hanging out—but never spending money—in their stores. These business owners had a few friends who shared their passion. The problem was they thought there were enough people who shared their passion to sustain their companies. Needless to say, neither of these would-be entrepreneurs is still in business.

Great businesses grow out of a need for their service or product. However, this need must be substantial and consistent enough to sustain a business. How do you know there's a viable market for your product? **Conduct your own market research**.

For example:

- Study research reports on the current market for your type of product/service in your sales area.
- Identify your potential competitors, and find out how they are performing in your sales area (sometimes called "competitive intelligence")
- Establish a test group beyond your immediate family and friends to discuss whether there is a real demand for your product or service.
- Be willing to adapt your product and its delivery to existing profitability requirements.

Business consultant Brian Tracy says, "For every dollar, for every hour that you put into research, you're going to save ten or twenty or thirty dollars or hours later on."[17]

TAKEAWAY:
There must be a demand for your service or product.

THOUGHTS TO CONSIDER:
1. If you ask 20 people if they need this product or service in the next thirty days, how many would say yes?
2. Ask yourself, with honesty, if your business idea is a personal interest or if it is a profitable idea that will appeal to many people?

ACTION STEP:
Take a survey of at least 20 people to confirm the need for your service or product idea.

KEEP YOUR BUSINESS MODEL SIMPLE

Is your business idea simple? I think your first business should be simple, if at all possible. Sometimes we over complicate our business model. In the planning stage, "a business model describes how your company creates, delivers and captures value. It is designed to change rapidly to reflect what you find outside the building in talking to customers."[18] Where entrepreneurs get into trouble, is that they over-reach, over-commit, and over-borrow. Start simple and stay simple.

Know what your customers want and figure out the most efficient way to provide it. Then make sure they keep coming back.

I recently ate at Waffle House. It's a good example of a company that has made the most of simplicity. Its menu is focused on primarily on a single meal (breakfast). Moreover, the menu reads like variations on a central theme. It's easy for a short order cook to prepare. It's also easy to serve.

Customers eat in a compact diner-style environment. Because a small wait crew can service it efficiently, wage costs are kept down. The truth is that you don't have to find and cultivate exceptional employees to manage a Waffle House. "Average" employees, who are plentiful, will do just fine.

By the way, this golden rule of simplicity isn't just a by-product of the mass consumer industry. Even industries that offer niche products have applied this rule successfully.

The fragrance company that produces "Clean" started with the premise that many consumers are attracted to a "fresh out of the shower" scent. It built a product line accordingly and is thriving at a time when more sophisticated perfume companies aren't.

To sum up: Start with a simple idea—and keep the execution simple, too. The simpler the operation, the lower your operating costs will be—and the higher your expected profits

TAKEAWAY:
Keep your business model simple.

THOUGHTS TO CONSIDER:
1. What is the simplest way you can provide your product or service?
2. What is the least expensive way to provide this?

ACTION STEP:
Streamline your business model so that an average employee can excel.

FILL A NEED OR MEET A DESIRE

I have read many books on how to build and grow businesses. But when you get down to it, your business will either need to fill a need or meet a desire.

Need-based businesses deal with products like food, housing, and clothing. Or basic services like plumbing, electricity, or auto repair. Want-based businesses often deal with the same goods or services but at a higher level of satisfaction and luxury.

For example, there is a big difference between eating at Denny's and eating out at an expensive restaurant. Any car can serve a functional need, like getting to work. A high-end luxury car or a sports car is more about comfort, wealth, and image.

As you begin drilling down into your proposed business idea, start evaluating whether it's a need or a desire that your business fulfills—or possibly some of both.

In your market research, evaluate how your market might shift depending on the precise mix of need and desire for your product or service. Startup mentor, Steve Blank, explains how to go about this: "You win in an existing market when you are better or faster on metrics that customers have told you are the basis of competition.... You gauge demand in an existing market by whether customers have told youthat they will switch, the cost they have told you it will take to acquire them and the amount of capital you can spend to do so."[19]

TAKEAWAY:

You are in business to fill a need or meet a desire/want.

THOUGHTS TO CONSIDER:

1. Is your business meeting a need? If so, which one(s)?
2. If your business fulfilling a desire? If so, which one(s)?

ACTION STEP:

Simply state again what need or desire your business is going to fill and who will be its customers.

FOCUS ON DURABLE GOODS AND SERVICES

You may remember the "dot com" bubble that crashed in the late 1990's. Companies that had no profit were worth hundreds of millions and even billions of dollars. Investors learned a very expensive lesson.

A company needs a product or service that is profitable, but also durable. Durability is another one of famed investor Warren Buffet's favorite qualities when investing in a company. So, as you would guess, he was not interested in investing in the Internet companies of the "dot com" era. He was criticized, but he had the last laugh. Do not get caught up in what is popular today.

There is always that rare company that initiates a new product or service, but it's an outlier. Don't over think business. In its simplest form you need a product/service people want with a price they are willing to pay that allows you to make the net profit you need to meet your financial goals.

To be successful, this product/service needs to be in demand for a long period of time. Think about what's durable, and how to make it better and more efficiently than anyone else.

Resist the siren song of "hot properties" and "quick kills." Master the fundamentals of start-up success. You can always venture out later with a solid track record and business foundation.

TAKEAWAY:
Think durable.

THOUGHTS TO CONSIDER:
1. Can you think of a company in your area that was popular for a short time but no longer exists because their product or service is no longer relevant?
2. Will your company's product or service be needed ten years from now?

ACTION STEP:
Read the list of Fortune 500 companies and highlight the ones that have a trendy product or service.

UNIQUE SELLING PROPOSITION

BusinessDictionary.com defines "Unique Selling Proposition" (USP) as "real or perceived benefit of a good or service that differentiates it from the competing brands and gives its buyer a logical reason to prefer it over other brands."[20] In short, ask yourself why someone would buy your product or service over your competition?

The answer to this question needs to be so clear and confident to you that you can recite it, defend it and bring a company that can do it into reality.

Your business idea should be extremely clear to you in why others will chose your company over your competition. When you have this clarity, it will make marketing—which we will discuss later—effective. A successful company must be one that is known by its ideal customer, liked and trusted and finally chosen and paid for its given product or service. This cycle must take place, and it is impossible to achieve this if you have a business from the beginning that does not have an honest unique selling proposition.

TAKEAWAY:
Unique selling proposition is why someone would choose your company over those offering a similar service or product.

THOUGHTS TO CONSIDER:
1. What benefit(s) is your company going to offer that your competition does not?
2. Do you believe these benefits are strong enough to make someone choose your company over your competition?

ACTION STEP:
What is your USP? Commit it to memory!

MODEL A FRANCHISE

I strongly considered buying a handyman franchise more than a decade ago. I saw that there was a great need in our area for a reputable handyman company. Moreover, after researching it, I learned of some very credible franchise opportunities.

Ultimately, though, I decided that a franchise was not a good fit for me. The company wanted me to service an area that was far too large. Being very familiar with the area, I knew that the radius they wanted me to service was actually four distinct areas. I felt that marketing to all of them would be prohibitively expensive.

Another problem I found was the over-sized office the company was offering. A whopping 400 square was unnecessary. I only saw the need for one desk for the person answering phones and distributing work orders. I would have been saddled with excessive overhead.

However, going through the process of considering a franchise did help me prepare to start my own business. The company's sales material answered questions that I had never even thought of. It just goes to show that researching opportunities and carefully weighing the pros and cons will usually yield dividends, regardless of what you decide.

I have no regrets about not purchasing the franchise. My business has since added services that I doubt the company would have allowed. We still do not service those other three areas because we haven't seen the need to.

In pursuit of possibly purchasing a franchise, I did learn things in my conversations, as well as studying their sales material, that I believe dramatically improved the initial success of my company. Franchises have done the homework and usually have a successful marketing strategy, competitive and profitable pricing, and an image that is considered professional looking by its customers. There may be a franchise you admire within your industry that can teach you something valuable prior to starting.

TAKEAWAY:

Franchises have done their homework so modeling the strengths of one should be considered.

THOUGHTS TO CONSIDER:

1. Can you duplicate legally a successful franchise without the costs and restrictions?
2. If there are franchises in your industry, what key qualities do they have?

ACTION STEP:

Consider using a credible franchise in the industry you are entering as a model to follow.

CONSIDER A FRANCHISE

You may want to own a successful business but the idea of starting something completely new frightens you. You know you want independence and the opportunity to control your schedule and income, but you have no original business ideas. In this case, your best bet may be to purchase a franchise.

Starting a franchise seems to be popular when someone gets a large settlement, many times from a downsizing buyout from his or her current employer.

Franchise companies simplify an industry and allow thousands of people to acquire ready-made businesses with an established infrastructure and a proven brand. One could cite countless examples. One is Auntie Anne's. The company took something as simple as making carnival-sized pretzels and turned it into a profitable business that anyone could operate.

The advantage of a franchise is that you get immediate legitimacy, as well as initial and on-going training, including marketing support. As you begin the process, it is best to find a business that is needed in your area.

Another advantage of franchises is that you normally do not need any experience in the industry you are entering. Additionally, by law the company must provide a Franchise Disclosure Document, which reveals how the company and their franchises are doing financially. It is a standard pre-sale disclosure document, and helps inform your decision.

You can expect to sign documents at some point to protect their trade secrets. The most important thing you can do is to speak with numerous franchisees, and not just the names they provide to you (likely the happiest franchise owners). I would go off the grid a bit and contact some owners whose names they have not provided.

TAKEAWAY:

Franchises are a great way to own your own business, especially if you don't have a new business idea in mind, and you have more than usual start-up capital available to you.

THOUGHTS TO CONSIDER:

1. Are you very independent and a creative thinker? If so, a franchise may not be a great fit for you.
2. Do you think you will benefit from initial and on-going training? If so, a franchise may be a good fit for you.

ACTION STEP:

Research franchise opportunities prior to starting your business if you think franchises are a good fit.

START A BUSINESS - OR PURCHASE ONE

Do you want to be a business owner or do you want to be an entrepreneur? Here's the difference: A business owner is someone who owns a business, while an entrepreneur is someone who starts a business.

The key word is *start*. I love the excitement of starting a business; I have started several over the years. However, I've found that purchasing an existing business is often the fastest way to reach my desired goal.

There are quite a few advantages to buying an existing business. You have the opportunity to look at existing financial records and customer lists. You may be able to speak with staff. You may already be familiar with the company. This removes many of the risks of starting a business.

Often times existing businesses are making money but could make a lot more with a few tweaks, such as more advertising and new enthusiasm. Also, you may be able to purchase a business for equal or less than what it takes to start a business.

Additionally, the owner may be willing to do some owner financing, which reduces your initial costs. Usually the asking price is in relation to how much the owner has personally made, or the gross receipts. Since most small businesses are S Corporations or an LLC, this figure is on their personal tax returns.

TAKEAWAY:

You may want to consider the option of buying an existing business before starting one.

THOUGHTS TO CONSIDER:

1. In order to reach your personal goals, do you need to start a new business or do you just want to own a profitable one?
2. Do you think your personal strengths are more suited for initiating or improving?

ACTION STEP:

Contact a business broker to see a listing of companies for sale. You can find business brokers in your local phone book or through an Internet search.

BUY THE COMPANY YOU WORK FOR

The traditional method of being an entrepreneur is to have an original idea that you turn into a business. As I have noted, you might also buy an existing business or purchase a franchise.

There is still another way. You can try to buy into—or buy out—the company you presently work for. I have personally allowed people to buy into my businesses. I have also seen friends buy the companies they work for. Allow me to explain.

I have a friend who worked for a small steel erection company whose owner was nearing retirement age. The owner had no transition plan to secure his company's future. My friend offered the owner a "buyout" plan. Not having any capital of his own, he offered to take profits from the company to purchase the business over time.

Here's an example of how this "buy-out" actually may work. Say, the current owner is presently making 100k per year. The buyer offers to pay the owner 50k for 10 years and 25k for another 5 years. The total payout is 625k. All of the monies come from the annual profits of the company.

For the owner this amounts to a 15-year retirement plan. For the "buyer," it's an opportunity to acquire a company without any start-up capital. The buyer continues to draw his regular salary, plus all new profit above expenses with the new innovations and energy they bring. The owner turns the company over to someone who knows all the ins and outs and can keep it running profitably. It's a win-win deal.

Caution: Under no circumstance should this be a "handshake" agreement. Have an attorney draw up the papers.

TAKEAWAY:

The best route in owning a business could possibly be buying the company you presently work for.

THOUGHTS TO CONSIDER:

1. Do you love the company and people you presently work for?
2. Are you the owner's most trusted employee, and do you have a close working relationship with them?

ACTION STEP:

Take the owner to lunch and ask, out of curiosity, whether they have a plan for ownership succession. (If they already have a relative already working for them, the answer may be obvious, so use common sense.)

REVIEW YOUR IDEA THOROUGHLY

I am the forever optimist and have a pretty high opinion of my potential, so it is hard for me to let go of what I think is a good business idea. What I mean by a business idea is this: A potential business that I think there is a need for and could be profitable.

My wife always jokes that I will make something work even if it is a bad idea. I have learned this is not always a good thing. What I do now is to let a business idea germinate for at least sixty days. To an entrepreneur, sixty days is an eternity. During this sixty day period I try to find all the reasons the business will not work. This is against my nature, being the optimist, but this practice has saved me a lot of money and later aggravation.

I look back at business ideas I had that seemed incredible the first week, but did not make the sixty-day cut, and in hindsight they were awful ideas.

I come up with about three to four business ideas a year that I genuinely believe are good. I pull the trigger on one of these ideas about every two years. If it is a good idea, it will pass the sixty-day test with flying colors. I have also found myself getting more motivated each day as I confirm that it is a good idea.

I now have a series of qualifying questions I ask myself whenever I come up with a new business idea.

TAKEAWAY:
Give your business idea a sixty-day test.

THOUGHTS TO CONSIDER:
1. Think very critically about why the business might not work.
2. Open your business idea up to criticism. Share the idea with others and get their opinion.

ACTION STEP:
Force yourself to make this business idea pass the sixty-day test.

DON'T QUIT YOUR DAY JOB

I want everyone to live a purposeful and passion-driven life, and I understand how owning your own business can bring this into reality. I, however, do not believe quitting your day job is always the best route to accomplish this. Determine exactly what you need to be involved with to make this new business a success.

Let me drill down on this: What specific tasks and responsibilities have you determined that you will personally be in charge of? I have started businesses where my key responsibilities were hiring, marketing, and setting the direction of the company. I was able to perform these functions before 8am and after 4pm, which allowed me to keep the very high paying job I held at the time. By keeping my day job and the guaranteed income, my stress level was much lower than if I had jumped into my new business full-time.

You can also begin part-time at your new start-up. Set measurable income goals for the company, and when you reach these is when you make the transition to full-time. This method has always motivated me since I had to grow the company to a certain level before joining its payroll. If you can maintain your current employment while starting this company, I think you should do it. Avoiding initial cash drain on the company is always a good idea.

TAKEAWAY:
You do not always have to quit your day job to start a business.

THOUGHTS TO CONSIDER:
1. Can you see any possible way to keep your present employment and effectively start a new business?
2. Would keeping your present employment—with its salary and possible benefits—reduce your stress level?

ACTION STEP:
List exactly what your responsibilities with your new business will be, and how much time will be required.

[3]

PLAN FOR SUCCESS

The lessons in this section will guide you through the ins and outs of a business plan. The three primary objectives of your business plan are to help you raise capital, confirm you have a profitable idea and provide an initial road map to follow during the first year or two. Keep it simple, and keep it honest. Don't worry if you still have questions after this chapter. Lessons in future sections—especially "Marketing Is Not Optional" and "Know Your Numbers"—will clarify some of the questions raised in this section, and will help you finalize your business plan.

OBTAIN COMPETITIVE INTELLIGENCE

An in-depth study of your competition is required in every business plan. I spend more time studying my potential competition than any other item in my preparation while starting a new business. I am like a general preparing for war. I want to know all their pricing. I want to know how they answer the phone and how they respond to leads. I will buy their product or use their services to gauge the quality. I know of no better way to establish what my competitive advantage will be until I know my competitors' weaknesses and strengths.

I have also had what I believed was a good potential business idea, but after obtaining my competition's pricing, I realized I could not make the net profit required to meet my income objective.

Do your due diligence in this area. The more you know about your competition the better prepared your company will be to capitalize on their weaknesses.

Author, John Christopher, crystallizes the importance of military intelligence: "The secret of success in battle lies often not so much in the use of one's own strength but in the exploitation of the other side's weaknesses."[21] The same could be said for competing in business.

TAKEAWAY:
You must know your competition's strengths and weaknesses.

THOUGHTS TO CONSIDER:
1. Who do you consider to be your top three competitors? Why?
2. Do you see the value of knowing your competition's strengths and weaknesses?

ACTION STEP:
Do a detailed competitor analysis to understand the strengths and weaknesses of all of your competitors.

OBTAIN BASELINE PRICING

One of the biggest reasons you should do detailed research on your competition is to obtain baseline pricing for your product or service. Pricing is crucial, especially in the beginning.

Sadly, some people fail to perform due diligence, and set a price that doesn't reflect their competitive advantage. When their pricing is too low, they end up with too little profit; when it's too high, they have too few customers. Either way, they lose out.

Sometimes, price competition is the most important aspect of your market. However, low product quality or a lack of professionalism in your market may allow you to set a higher price, and still be highly competitive. It just depends.

For example, a few years back, I called Furniture Medic to fix a theater chair I had. The competition for fixing furniture was scattered between the handyman market and furniture stores. Furniture Medic had established itself as the authority on fixing furniture and was able to charge higher prices. I readily agreed to pay the company more in exchange for its superior craftsmanship.

I'm not a psychologist, but the price of your product or service says something about you. Sometimes a potential customer will see the lowest price and wonder if that price comes from cheap manufacturing or bare-bones services. Charging the least can lose you business unless you are Wal-Mart. Tim Berry, founder of Palo Alto Software, tells this story, "I lost a consulting job I really wanted once when I bid $25k for it and a competitor bid $75k. The guy who gave me the bad news told me everybody liked my proposal, but they wanted the best, so they went for the higher price."[22]

If you have competition, that means your prices have to be competitive, but not the lowest. So do your research before quoting a price.

TAKEAWAY:
Establishing correct pricing is critical to profit.

THOUGHTS TO CONSIDER:
1. What is the average pricing of your three biggest competitors?
2. Is there something totally new you can bring to this industry that allows you to charge more?

ACTION STEP:
Based on the answers to the above questions, set your pricing, and see if it meets your net profit goal.

DEFINE YOUR COMPETITIVE ADVANTAGE

In sports, you maximize your strengths and exploit your opponents' weaknesses, as a common and effective strategy for victory.

The same is true in business. Your business must be superior to your competitors in at least one area. In business, typically, the areas to focus on are customer service, quality, price, and speed. For example: Rolex offers quality; Nordstrom offers exceptional customer service; Wal-Mart provides products at lower costs; McDonalds is known for its ability to serve food quickly in a clean environment; Fed-Ex is known for its fast delivery service of parcels.

What is your company superior at? Why should a customer choose your company over another? If you don't know the answer to this question, then you should not be starting this company. Your competitive advantage can be broad in its scope, but these qualities are musts for success. I would also warn against customer service being your competitive advantage, as most companies think they are providing superior customer service compared to their competition. This is also an area that will take the longest, normally, to bear fruit.

Catalog merchant, Lillian Hochberg, puts the case this way: "Don't try to be all things to all people. Concentrate on selling something unique that you know there is a need for, offer competitive pricing and good customer service." Former General Electric CEO, Jack Welch, says it even more simply: "If you don't have a competitive advantage, don't compete."

TAKEAWAY:

You must be superior in a key area: price, speed, quality, more options and uses, and finally, customer service.

THOUGHTS TO CONSIDER:

1. Can you be superior in quality or provide your product/service at a lower cost?
2. Are you able to provide your product or service faster than your competition?

ACTION STEP:

On the front-end, figure out what it will take to be either faster, higher quality, or less expensive than your competitor. You have to be one (or more) to have a competitive advantage.

MISSION STATEMENT

If you are seeking investment dollars from anyone, including your network of family and friends, you will be prepared to provide a detailed business plan. And one of the items within the business plan is your mission statement. Even if you do not need an outside penny to start your company, I think you should spend some time creating a mission statement anyway.

A mission statement declares the purpose of your company. I have heard it said it should fit on a T-shirt or the back of a business card. Therefore, it does not need to be long but needs to be stated concisely. Your mission statement declares the purpose of your company (what will it do or provide) and who is the target customer. It will then state how you will provide value to your customers. It may also proclaim your distinction. It may not necessarily have all three of these in it but it will include at least two. I believe if customers read it, and believed you could perform what it commits to, they would want to use, or buy from, your company.

Key Components:

1. Who is your target customer/key market?
2. What will you do or provide to you target market/key customer?
3. What makes your product or service unique?
4. What value will you provide to your target customer/key market?

For example, McDonald's mission is, "To provide the fast food customer food prepared in the same high-quality manner worldwide that is tasty, reasonably-priced and delivered consistently in a low-key decor and friendly atmosphere." The mission statement we use for one of our companies is, "To provide workmanship that exceeds our customers' expectations in a timely and professional manner." I wrote this before we ever opened our doors for business. This mission gives my employees a clear direction on the quality of work I want them to perform.

TAKEAWAY:

A mission statement will be the overriding daily goal of your company.

THOUGHTS TO CONSIDER:

1. What product or service are you providing, and who is your target customer? For example, McDonald's target customer is people who eat fast food.
2. What is going to be distinct about your product or service? McDonald's food will be prepared in high-quality manner, reasonably prices and delivered consistently.

ACTION STEP:

Find mission statements for companies you respect, and your competitors. Create the mission statement for your company.

VISION STATEMENT

Another valuable declaration in your planning is your vision statement. Mission statements focus on what the company does and how well it does it. Vision statements articulate what you want the company to become. If you could see your company five years from now, what would it look like and be known for? Susan Ward, in About.com says, "It is a picture of your company in the future." It should serve as inspiration to you and your employees.

Like mission statements, vision statements are also included in a business plan when seeking outside funding. If you were going to family and friends for funding, it would still be good to include a vision statement.

One example of a vision statement is: "To be Central Virginia's leading provider of residential water treatment systems." This statement may evolve over time as you add new products and services. It should be brief and succinct. It should provide a written declaration of your highest goal as a company. If you achieved this, and only this as a company, you would be satisfied.

Your company's reputation is built on a foundation of your first customers, and a vision statement provides your performance standard for your employees in the first critical days. Think of it this way: "You want missionaries, not mercenaries—passionate, manically-focused founders who believe in a vision."[23] This vision should motivate you and your employees each day. And it should be posted so that it is viewed daily.

Once you have a vision statement, you have a target. Now what actions will you need to take to accomplish this vision? Your vision statement will dictate the type of employee you will need to accomplish this vision. What quality product or service will be provided and what will it take to provide this?

This is what separates average companies from great companies. Great companies have an ambitious vision, and with this vision, they have a commitment to take the necessary action steps to accomplish it.

TAKEAWAY:
Your vision statement is your highest goal as a company.

THOUGHTS TO CONSIDER:
1. If you only accomplished one thing this year, as a company, what would you want it to be?
2. If you have no limitations and could accomplish anything in the next five years, what would you want it to be?

ACTION STEP:
Write your company's vision statement.

VALUE STATEMENT

Your value statement is the last piece of your company's declarations. The value statement is a set of core beliefs your company will operate by. These normally reflect the personal values of the owner or founder. For example, it should be obvious to anyone who goes to a Chick-Fil-A on a Sunday and finds it closed, that the founder, S. Truett Cathy, had a set of values that prioritized going to church on Sunday over work and making a profit. A value statement will provide guiding principles and beliefs that should influence the behavior of those who work within a given company.

You will have many opportunities to turn a profit, some of which will violate your core values. Enron is just one example of a company whose key leadership lost sight of a set of beliefs that I'm sure the company had. Another example would be, if you value saving the planet in regard to global warming, you would have something in your value statement reflecting this view and your practices would in turn be environmentally friendly.

Values statements are generally longer than mission or vision statements. If the latter typically run a sentence or two (at most), a value statement is usually an entire paragraph. It may even use bullet points or sub-titles to list or enumerate the company's core beliefs. The value statement may be as simple as the following example:

"Our company is guided by four core beliefs:

- **Integrity** (honesty and transparency in all business and customer relationships)
- **Social responsibility** (respect for diversity and non-discrimination)
- **Profitability** (determination to grow the company and expand our operations)
- **Excellence** (commitment to providing the very best product on the market)."

As I hope you can see, your vision statement should align with your value statement. There is no wrong value statement, assuming you intend to conduct business legally. It is just the core principles that will guide you.

TAKEAWAY:
Your value statement is your company's moral compass.

THOUGHTS TO CONSIDER:
1. What company values are you familiar with and have respect for?
2. What personal values do you have that will guide your company?

ACTION STEP:
Write your company's value statement.

FINANCING YOUR START-UP

One of the most popular sources of outside capital for starting a business is an "angel investor," usually one or more members of your family or close friends. I also believe they need to be able to afford to lose the money if your business does not succeed.

Don't get me wrong: They wouldn't be happy if your business fails, but they also wouldn't lose their house over it. Keep in mind, though, your relationship with them can still be damaged if your business doesn't work out and you are unable to pay them back.

Your first step is to schedule an appointment to see your prospective "angel." In advance of the meeting, tell this person that you are considering starting a business. This will usually prepare them that you may be seeking some funding. When you meet with them, speak clearly and confidently. What you must communicate to any potential investors—both within your business plan and verbally in a meeting—is that they will get their money back with a nice return on their investment. But don't overdo it: "Under-promise and over-deliver, not the other way around."[24]

I always prefer to borrow start-up capital and give a generous return when starting a company rather than giving stock. Stock lasts forever and I have found that making a dividend payment year after year can become expensive.

If, however, you need to raise a great deal of money, you may need to consider stock. You can speak with your accountant or lawyer on how best to issue stock. Knowing whether you are going to issue stock is also something you need to know before starting the business, as this will dictate what type of corporation will best suit your needs.

TAKEAWAY:

Investors need to know the details of your business plan, especially how and when they will get a return on their investments.

THOUGHTS TO CONSIDER:

1. Are you willing to risk the relationship with this potential investor if things don't work out?
2. Ask yourself: If you had the money and someone presented this business idea to you, with the same terms, would you invest?

ACTION STEP:

Practice presenting your investment proposal to a few people prior to giving it to the individuals from whom you are seeking capital.

DON'T COUNT ON VENTURE CAPITAL

Let me make this clear: You are not creating a business plan because you think you're going to get venture capital. Only a very small percentage of start-up firms (less than 1%) get their initial capital from this source, either wealthy investors or an investment bank. That translates into 1,500 companies of the nearly 500,000 that start up each year.

Moreover, the competition for venture capital funding is fierce, but the number of venture capitalists is relatively small. A typical venture capitalist might review 400 proposals per year and fund 1. Statistically speaking, this is like finding a needle in the proverbial haystack.

Venture capital takes a substantial risk with the hope for a large gain. This group will often take an equity position in the company and may involve themselves in key company decisions. The fact is that some start-ups need substantial initial capital because they are bringing an invention into market. They may also be introducing a new industry, or an improvement in an existing industry.

A great example of venture capital is a new hit show (and who knows how long it will last), called *Shark Tank*. In the show, someone has what they believe is a great idea and needs funding, they have maybe 2 minutes to present their business proposal to a panel of investors. I have noticed that it is new inventions that gain the most attention by the panel of sharks (investors) seeking to invest.

Venture capital has its place, and many companies that have become household names required such capital. This type of initial investment capital, however, only accounts for a fraction of 1% of all start-up companies, so it would be foolish to think this will be initial funding you can count on.

TAKEAWAY:

Venture Capital is applicable to a slight minority of start-up companies; so do not count on it.

THOUGHTS TO CONSIDER:

1. Did you think you were going to get venture capital? If so, did you expect it to be like applying for a loan?
2. Does your business idea require substantial initial investment?

ACTION STEP:

Plan on getting your funding from someone other than a venture capital firm. (Based on statistics)

CREATE A BUSINESS PLAN

Regardless of whether you need outside financing or not, a business plan is an important step in planning your business. The business plan not only allows you to become crystal clear about how your company will operate profitably, it allows potential funders to decide whether your company might be worth investing in.

If the thought of writing a lengthy business plan overwhelms you, begin with answering the questions below. Answering these questions will establish your initial road map. Some of the answers will become clearer in chapters to follow.

- What will your business do?
- What research confirms there is a demand for your business in the market?
- Who will be your competition and what are their strengths/weaknesses?
- What is your competitor's pricing?
- What will be your pricing?
- What will be your competitive advantage(s) and distinctions? (Why customers will choose you.)
- Who is your ideal customer and how are you going to market to them?
- Develop a one-year marketing plan
- What skills and expertise will you need to hire?
- What will be all the costs to operate this business per week and month?
- What will be your conservative projected gross and net income per week and month?
- Is your net income enough to pay you the income you wish to make? If it is not, you must either have more customers, or charge more for your product/service.
- Create a mission, vision, and value statement.
- Create one-year, three-year, and five-year goals for your company.

Starting a business requires discipline. The same discipline it takes to do a business plan.

Bruce Bachenheimer, professor at Pace University, asks, "Would you enter a high-stakes poker tournament without knowing the game, assuming that you'll figure it out as you go?"[25]

TAKEAWAY:
Your business plan is meant to establish whether or not you should go forward with this business idea.

THOUGHTS TO CONSIDER:
1. If you do not have the time and discipline to do a business plan, you should not go into business.
2. Can you see the value in answering these questions?

ACTION STEP:
Answer the questions in detail, and you now have a simple but effective business plan.

MAKE AN EXHAUSTIVE LIST OF PRE-LAUNCH TASKS

The father of modern education, John Dewey wrote, "Arriving at one goal, is the starting point to another."[26] And now that you have a business plan that has confirmed that you have a potential to make the income you wish, the next step is actually starting the business. I have started businesses from retail to service and many in between. Without exception, the next step was to formulate an exhaustive list of every possible thing that needed to be done prior to "turning the lights on" and serving the first paying customer.

Here are some of the key areas, each of which will contain multiple tasks. Each business and industry will contain different items on this list, but this is a general list to get you on the right track.

- Name, Tagline, Domain
- Incorporating
- Licensing and Permits
- Banking
- Website
- Physical Location
- Signage
- Phone Number
- Forms, Stationary, Office Supplies
- Machinery, Tools, Products, etc.
- Professional Needs
- Staffing Needs
- Uniforms
- Miscellaneous

The first man to reach the North and South poles, Roald Admundsen said, "Adventure is just bad planning," so roll up your sleeves and sort out the nuts and bolts before you launch. Never forget this: "The goal is not just to launch, but to launch a successful company."[27]

TAKEAWAY:

You must know everything you need to have done before you can service your first customer.

THOUGHTS TO CONSIDER:

1. What items come to mind as you make your list? The longer the list, the better, but do not get overwhelmed.
2. Can you think of a project you once had that seemed overwhelming at first but you succeeded at?

ACTION STEP:

Formulate your list of items that need to be done before you can open your doors, and put a deadline next to each item.

CONSIDER THE BEST LAUNCH SEASON

I am of the mindset that cash is like oxygen in business. Moreover, starting a business at the wrong time of year is just wasting money. It is your job to know the peak and low times for the business that you are entering. I am not saying that you must time it to the day, but you do not open a seasonal business in the off-season.

If you do not know the peak seasons of the business you are entering, then call a similar business an hour or two away. I have driven to other cities, walked in, and talked to management of similar businesses that I was considering starting. If you call and ask to speak with the owner and introduce yourself as a business owner, the respondent will usually take your call. I have found calling and speaking to other owners, in other areas, with a similar business, to be a valuable resource. If they do not view you as competition, they will usually help.

The best launch season may also be related to your personal situation. If you are 2-3 years away from a retirement package or 2-3 months from a bonus, you may want to stay put and mothball your company.

I love chasing a dream, but rarely does success follow stupidity. Other personal considerations are the expected birth of a child, a child's entry into college, or a lingering personal or family illness that may require time away from the company.

Alternatively, if the market is ripe, you could start the company with someone else temporarily at the helm. This course has risks, but if you already have a business partner, it could be managed. Some time you do need to strike while the market is especially hot, or simply open to new entrants.

TAKEAWAY:
Think like a general going to war. What is the best time to strike?

THOUGHTS TO CONSIDER:
1. Are you starting a seasonal business?
2. Are you leaving your present employment at the best time?

ACTION STEP:
Plan your grand opening as if you only had 30 days to run this business.

ADAPT TO CHANGING CIRCUMSTANCES

You start a business with a plan, but like any good leader, you are smart enough to change the plan quickly when you see something not working. Or maybe you see something working well that you didn't expect to work. This does not mean you are scrapping your business plan a month in, but that you are alert to the fact that things may evolve that you did not expect.

For example, you may start a roofing company with the goal of offering the most cost effective complete roof replacements in the area. Let's say, within the first three months of starting, your city receives a strong series of storms that damage roofs throughout your service area. The phone calls you receive are for repairs, not for complete replacements. If you are smart, you turn on a dime and position your company to seize this opportunity. You may come to discover that there are very few companies doing simple to mid-level roof repairs in your area. You see this new opportunity and add roof repairs to your list of services your company performs.

Bill Gates, founder of Microsoft, placed enormous emphasis on the ability of companies to adapt. "A company's ability to respond to an unplanned event, good or bad, is a prime indicator of its ability to compete," he says.

Internet investor, Ajaero Tony Martins, writes: "Your greatest and most powerful business survival strategy is going to be the speed at which you handle the speed of change. That speed of change is trend."

Even as a new business owner, you need to stay alert and operate nimbly. Opportunities may rise that were not part of your original business planning. Don't be afraid to seize them.

TAKEAWAY:
Be flexible with your business and seize opportunities that come your way.

THOUGHTS TO CONSIDER:
1. What additional products or services could you offer with a simple modification?
2. Could you offer this new service or product within thirty days?

ACTION STEP:
Have a list of new products or services you could bring to the marketplace quickly.

[4]

PROTECT YOURSELF AND YOUR BUSINESS

There are a lot of things to do in the start-up phase of your business. It is important that you consider all the ways to protect yourself—and your business—as you get started. From incorporation to insurance to intellectual property, the lessons in this section help you take steps needed to protect yourself and your business.

INCORPORATE YOUR BUSINESS

The owner of a corporation doesn't carry as much liability as a Sole Proprietor, both legally and financially. BizFilings, a small business incorporation-consulting firm, lays out the benefits, "Creditors can't pursue your home or car to pay business debts. And corporations often gain tax advantages, writing off such things as health insurance premiums, savings on self-employment taxes, and life insurance."[28] Other advantages are enhanced credibility, potential for growth, and it will be easier to sell your business.

There are three types of corporations you might consider when starting your company: C Corp, S Corp, and Limited Liability Company (LLC).

In short, C Corp is for larger companies that sell stock in their company and have over 100 shareholders. S Corp businesses can sell stock but have no more than 100 shareholders. The LLC, which has always been the preferred choice for small businesses, does not have stock but pass all profits and losses to personal income. S Corp is similar to an LLC as the profits and losses are passed on to the business owner's personal tax return.

Why incorporate? And why incorporate before you start operating your business? Being a corporation gives you protection against someone suing you personally. It also allows you to put debt in the company's name and get it off your personal credit report. In the beginning, you will still be securing most things personally, but in time this will change. It is wise to consult your accountant or lawyer in deciding what would be the best choice for your business.

If you already know what type of corporation will best suit your needs, you can incorporate yourself by calling your state corporation commission and requesting the needed forms. It is a simple process and can also be done online.

TAKEAWAY:

Incorporate your business before you start.

THOUGHTS TO CONSIDER:

1. You can go online and begin reading about the type of corporation best fits your situation.
2. Consider spending the money to meet with an accountant or lawyer for an hour or two and get professional advice.

ACTION STEP:

Apply to be a corporation.

PURCHASE INSURANCE

It is a mistake to think you save money by having the bare minimum or no insurance at all. Blogger and insurance agent, Ryan Hanley writes, "Forgetting about Insurance is like walking the tight rope without a net. You might be the best tightrope walker in the world, but one gust of wind and all your practice and work doesn't mean squat."[29] Insurance keeps you in business—as it only takes one catastrophe to bankrupt the business.

Industry associations may offer a group discount on various types of insurance. You may be aware of the standard policies needed such as worker's compensation and general liability, but you should also consider getting a personal and business umbrella policy. It gives a final layer of protection. If, for some reason, the policies you have in place do not cover the claim, the umbrella policy provides additional coverage.

These umbrella policies are very inexpensive and can give great peace of mind. Transitioning your business upon death through life insurance that pays your estate is also usually done through insurance. Another policy to consider is an employment practices policy that, in short, provides protection against an employee suing you for sexual harassment or wrongful termination.

To protect yourself and your family, you can purchase a health insurance plan with a very high deductible so that at least you have some protection. A high deductible plan allows you to have insurance in the event that something happens, but it will not cost much per month. These plans usually give you a discounted price that the insurance company pays on services and prescriptions.

TAKEAWAY:

It is important to get business insurance to protect yourself, and your business, in the case of unforeseen events.

THOUGHTS TO CONSIDER:

1. What are the needed policies that apply to the business you are entering into?
2. Ask business owners you respect about their insurance broker.

ACTION STEP:

Meet with an insurance broker and obtain the needed insurance for yourself and your business

PROTECT YOUR INTELLECTUAL PROPERTY

Intellectual property in business usually refers to a name, logo, trade secret, or invention. It is the result of someone's creativity. It has value and must be protected. You can look at nearly any product to see trademarks. For example, Coca Cola's "Coke," shown with a small "r" inside a circle, is a registered trademark. The Coca Cola brand and the word Coke is recognizable, and carries with it substantial value to its owner. This is a simple illustration of intellectual property (IP).

Other common types of intellectual property include copyrights, patents, industrial design rights, and trade secrets, which apply in some jurisdictions. Trademarking, trade secrets, and patents seem to be the ones that apply most in businesses. There are subtle but important differences between these types of protection that you need to learn and apply to your specific business situation.

The vital reason to have intellectual property protected is that it adds real value to your company—value that someone can invest in. We all recognize the value of real estate, but intellectual property is equally valuable. Zwilling emphasizes, "Intellectual property is also often the largest element of early-stage company valuations for professional investors."[30] IP rights protect unique aspects of your company that give it a competitive advantage, especially while trying to keep an edge against bigger, established competition. They make it possible for you to license or franchise part or all of your operations, should you choose to. IP rights prevent others from unfairly encroaching upon you.

The process of applying for intellectual property protection is simple and can start with an Internet search of "how to trademark" or "how to patent." Sometimes it is as simple as paying a fee and registering your intellectual property with the proper authorities. Make sure you add the appropriate trademark (tm) or copyright (c) symbols to your business communications, including your advertising and signage, to discourage unscrupulous copycats. It will also lend public credibility to your business.

TAKEAWAY:
Protect your creative ideas using intellectual property protection.

THOUGHTS TO CONSIDER:
1. Are you going to have a one-of-a-kind logo or tagline?
2. Are you going to have a unique recipe or invention?

ACTION STEP:
Take all needed steps to protect anything your have determined is intellectual property..

IF YOU PARTNER, CONSIDER THESE RULES

If you have chosen a partnership, there are some rules to follow. Sadly, I have learned all these rules the expensive way.

Going into a business partnership is very similar to a marriage. In fact, you will spend more time talking to and being around this person than your spouse, in the beginning. You need to know what buttons set each other off. For instance, I had a partner who did not have a college education and anything that implied he was not smart would set him off. I was always careful to never imply I was smarter just because I went to college. He was a great guy who taught me a lot about the industry we were in, but like everybody, he had things that set him off.

Treat the partnership agreement like a "pre-nup." Negotiate what the buyout would be well before you start this business. I recommend if either partner decides to leave the business on his/ her own in the first three years, that partner receive nothing more than the money they put in. This money should also be returned with favorable terms to the existing partner, as you don't want to get hit with owning a large sum of money out of the blue. I have had to buy partners out with very little notice and it has crippled me financially.

It is best to write out the basic terms of your partnership agreement and have it reviewed by an attorney. Ann Logue, of Entrepreneur Magazine, drives this home, "Partners often hold off on putting key terms in writing...when everyone is enthusiastic and in sync.... But having basic partnerships that outline each party's role and obligations...is key to preventing problems down the road."[31] A non-compete agreement should also be included in this partnership agreement. If you cannot afford an attorney, at the very least, get this agreement notarized.

TAKEAWAY:

Prepare terms for a buyout prior to being formal business partners.

THOUGHTS TO CONSIDER:

1. Do you know what pushes your partner's buttons?
2. Do you plan to have a lawyer review your partnership agreement?

ACTION STEP:

Put in writing the terms of your partnership agreement, including buyout terms and non-compete agreements.

ESTABLISH THE PROPER LEGAL FRAMEWORK

You need to be aware of all needed licenses, permits, and certifications for the industry you are entering. You can usually find these out by going to your local business tax office or contacting your local Chamber of Commerce. Ignorance is not an excuse, so contact whomever necessary to find out what is required to do business in your industry and in your area.

When you start your business, you may have a partner or key employee that has all the needed licenses to operate your business. For what it is worth, this leaves you in a very vulnerable position if this person should ever leave.

If at all possible, obtain all the licenses yourself as soon as you can. Don't wait. Failure to obtain all of the proper licenses can prevent you from opening your doors on your anticipated target date. Remember: government bureaucracies can be painfully slow. Allow for additional time beyond the timeframes stated when obtaining the licenses you need.

The most important licenses to consider initially are the following:

- Local licenses, permits and registrations
- Employer Identification Number, or EIN
- Professional licenses
- State tax license
- State labor department registration (required by most, but not all, states)
- Liquor license (only as applicable)

TAKEAWAY:

You must have all the needed licenses, permits, and certifications for your industry.

THOUGHTS TO CONSIDER:

1. Do you know all the licenses, permits, and certifications required in your line of business?
2. Do any of these require a test that may delay your start date?

ACTION STEP:

Find out what licenses, permits, and certifications are required and obtain them prior to starting your business.

KNOW ALL APPLICABLE LABOR LAWS

Many business owners howl at the amount of "government red tape" that seems to complicate our operations. However, nothing will get you into more trouble faster than failing to abide by federal, state and local labor laws. Here are 4 areas that you should keep abreast of:

- **Hiring discrimination.** Under federal law, you cannot hire employees based only on their gender, race, ethnicity, marital status, or sexual orientation. That means you need to interview prospective employees in ways that do not suggest that you might be choosing them based on these criteria. If certain jobs require people with specific skills, make sure your criteria are legal.
- **Child labor.** Under the Fair Labor Standards Act, it is unlawful to employ children younger than 14 in non-agricultural occupations. Children 14-15 can be employed outside school hours for limited periods of time. 16- and 17-year-olds can be hired in any occupation other than those deemed "hazardous."
- **Independent contractors.** The IRS has established guidelines to determine whether an employee is a regular employee (part-time or full-time) or a contract worker. Some employers have abused the distinction by attempting to hire most of their workers as contractors. If your employees work for you on a regular schedule at your place of business, they would normally be classified as regular employees.
- **Immigration law.** Businesses must keep an up-to-date "I-9" form—which verifies a worker's legal citizenship or immigration status—on file for every employee. (I-9 forms are not required of applicants, just employees.) Keep I-9 forms on file for 7 years after employment is severed.

Keep in mind that these are federal standards; each state typically has its own labor laws. For further information, contact an attorney or the National Federation of Independent Business (NFIB). If you become an NFIB member, you will have access to its free labor law hotline.

TAKEAWAY:
Stay abreast of all federal, state or local labor laws that might affect the operations of your business.

THOUGHTS TO CONSIDER:
1. Do you know all the hiring, and employment laws and penalties that govern the operations of your business?
2. Have you considered having an attorney review your compliance with these laws?

ACTION STEP:
Find out if your local SBA, or another group, is offering a free workshop on the labor (and other) laws governing the operations of small businesses. (Laws continue to change so stay current)

[5]

BUILD A SUCCESSFUL TEAM

When starting a business, your team consists of staff, professional advisors, and mentors. Building a successful team is one of the most important things that will lead to your business' success. In this section, you will learn how to find, and surround yourself with people who will support your idea, respect your leadership, who you will work well with, and who will provide helpful guidance.

QUALIFY YOUR LABOR MARKET

When you are deciding what kind of business to start, think twice before you pick a business where hiring is harder than finding a rocket scientist. What do I mean? If you choose a business that requires an expertise or skill that you yourself don't have, obviously you will need to hire someone who has that skill. Make sure you can find and hire such a person within no more than three days. If you can't, the employee has you hostage and will eventually know it. As a rule, it is hard to grow when you cannot hire quickly. HR expert, Carolyn Hughes, of SimplyHired.com insists that hiring qualified employees on the fly is the key to sustained growth: "A company can only grow as fast as it can hire great people. Your success as a business depends upon your commitment to the hiring process. The benefits of finding great people who fit with your company culture, share your vision and make an immediate and lasting impact cannot be understated."[32] Also beware of any professional certifications that the business you are entering may require.

In simple terms, if you are starting an electrical service company, there needs to be an electrician on your staff. I recently wanted to start an appliance repair business. I knew there was a need, as there were very few companies to choose from in our area offering this service. I was as excited about starting this business as any in the past. Then I ran some help wanted ads. It was close to impossible to find someone with the manufacturer certifications needed to work on the various brand appliances. I knew from experience that I would not start this business when hiring an appliance repairperson was such a huge stumbling block.

By the way, be aware of possible labor supply issues when it comes to lower skilled workers, too. In some labor markets, you may encounter shortages of these workers, especially during particular seasons. Above all, be aware of what your labor pool actually looks like. Placing ads will give you some indication. However, you might want to contact the local Chamber of Commerce and talk with other business owners about the labor supply challenges they have encountered.

TAKEAWAY:

You must be able to hire the skill you need quickly and easily.

THOUGHTS TO CONSIDER:
1. What skills do your employees need?
2. Where will you find these skilled individuals?

ACTION STEP:

Run an ad (online for free) and see how easy it is to get applicants for this area of skills needed.

TRY TO HIRE THE BEST, REGARDLESS

Make it your mission to surround yourself with the most talented, smartest, experienced and competent team of employees you can find—and make sure you actually look for them. Sadly, it is all too common for new business owners to hire family members and friends, either out of a sense of obligation or by default. Some owners also assume—wrongly—that these intimates will be "loyal" and more readily accept their direction. Like nearly all "lazy" solutions, this one can easily backfire.

Try to hire staff that is outside your immediate comfort zone. The main criterion is whether they will add value to your company. Do not be intimidated or threatened because someone is older with twenty years more experience than you. In this setting, you may sometimes feel like you are working for one of your own employees. However, if you hire this person in the right spirit, he or she can be a real asset, as studies show that more mature employees "can be more reliable, punctual, aware of safety, better at avoiding disciplinary actions and have better attendance."[33]

Let more experienced employees know that you value their input, but expect their full support for the decisions that you alone are authorized to make. Remember—and don't be afraid to gently remind them—you're the boss.

A good illustration of how this relationship can work is in the NFL. Typically, the head coach of a football team has numerous assistants, many of whom have been head coaches themselves. Often, these "assistants" have far more football experience than the head coach does. However, the head coach still makes all key decisions.

I will never forget when former NFL coach Dick Vermeil came back to coaching after an early retirement (he was in his 40s when he retired from the Philadelphia Eagles in the early 1980s). He came back nearly 20 years later and assembled an all-star coaching staff. It was the oldest coaching staff in football in terms of its combined experience. Yes, you guessed it: Vermeil's new team went on to win the Super Bowl.

TAKEAWAY:
Hire the most talented and experienced staff you possibly can afford.

THOUGHTS TO CONSIDER:
1. If you have been in a position to hire people in your past, have you always hired the most talented people you could?
2. Can you see value in hiring someone with more experience than you?

ACTION STEP:
Commit to hiring the best staff possible.

THERE ARE MECHANICS TO HIRING

Interviewing and hiring may seem simple, but the process requires preparation and forethought. Here is a list of some simple mechanics to consider:

- Be clear what you are looking for in your ad. Be specific with duties and expectations listed.
- Have a list of questions printed out before the interview. This will keep you on point and establishes professionalism. It is important to go over the job title and duties, and your expectations, in the initial interview.
- Let each candidate know that whomever you hire will get a thirty-day trial period. I have had too many people tell me they can do a job that they simply cannot do. Telling them there is a trial period tends to keep them more honest with their assessment of their own abilities.
- Conduct all the interviews over one or two days. This makes it easier to compare candidates. If the hiring is prolonged, you may lose a good early candidate or be more tempted to go with one you interviewed most recently.
- I cannot stress this next point enough: Do not hire anyone the day you interview him or her, if at all possible. I do recognize that some positions just need to be filled with a warm body, but if it is more than this, sleep on it. I cannot tell you how many times my mind has changed with a night's rest.
- I said this earlier but it bears repeating. Never, ever, ask interviewees their age, marital status, parenting status, religion or political views, as this opens you up for discrimination issues.

TAKEAWAY:
There is a process that needs to be followed for great hiring.

THOUGHTS TO CONSIDER:
1. Have you ever interviewed and hired employees?
2. When possible, ask for the opinion of other trusted employees or business associates. If they know the person being interviewed, they may have some important insights to add.

ACTION STEP:
Develop a series of interview questions, along with a job description and duties, for all positions you are hiring.

APPROACH STAFFING STRATEGICALLY

Think of everyone you might possibly need to operate your business on a day-in, day-out basis. Are all of these positions full-time? Next, define their functional roles, and start writing job descriptions.

You also need to define what your ideal employee looks and sounds like. This goes beyond functional role. How well might a prospective staff person embody the goals and principles of your company as reflected in your mission and value statements? To one degree or another, every employee is a walking-and-talking company representative. Those with direct and sustained contact with your customers should strongly reflect your company's business ethos.

You should prepare a series of interview questions that give you a good "read" on each individual. Create a process by which you can determine reliability, attitude, and competence, as well as more intangible personality assets (e.g., "likeability") that might enhance their value. A staff that is dull, unreliable, lacks competence, and has a sub-par work ethic is a sure-fire recipe for disaster.

As you interview different candidates, you might also ask yourself these questions.

- First, is this someone you would enjoy spending a workday with? The fact is that even if it's not you, someone is going to spend the workday with him or her.
- Second, will the employees I have chosen make a good "team"? It's hard to know for sure in advance, and there is no single recipe for success. However, give some thought to creating a balance of aptitudes and personality types.
- Third, never, ever choose employees on the basis of their race, ethnicity, gender or perceived sexual orientation. Your customer base is very likely diverse and your staff should reflect that diversity. It's not just the right thing. It's also good for business.

- Fourth, know the law. Read up on basic rules for non-discriminatory hiring, and use that to shape the way you ask questions. Consulting an attorney can help, and could also insulate you from any claim that you might have unintentionally engaged in hiring discrimination.

TAKEAWAY:
Your staffing choices are a reflection of your business. Give strategic thought to who you hire.

THOUGHTS TO CONSIDER:
1. What level of competency do you need at each staff position?
2. What mix of staff will make for the most effective, value-enhancing team?

ACTION STEP:
Interview and hire your team.

IF YOU DON'T HAVE THE SKILLS, PARTNER

I love those television commercials where people think they're fit to do something for which they have no training simply because they stayed at a Holiday Inn Express. It was a great marketing campaign that still sticks in my mind.

In Chapter 1, I laid out criteria for qualifying yourself as a business owner. You might think that having a strong background in the industry that you're planning to enter is essential. Not necessarily. If you can find a partner with the background you lack, you may be more prepared than you realize.

I started a home improvement company without knowing the difference between a flathead and a Phillips screwdriver. Because I lacked industry expertise, I brought on a partner with twenty years of experience in the business. It would lead to 3 divisions and millions in revenue. His industry background and my marketing skills were the perfect complement of talents needed to succeed with this new business. This also includes the "soft" skills of business, like personality. For example, "An optimist needs a pessimist to temper the rose-colored glasses with reality. And a shy person needs someone more outgoing to handle the 'people' part of running a business," according to Rieva Lesonsky, CEO and President of GrowBiz Media.[34]

Keep in mind, though, that these partnerships must be solidly based. You need to learn the business in your own right, and your partner, however experienced, won't have all the answers. Make sure your partnership agreement clarifies how business decisions are to be made. In the end, a partnership is a mutual learning experience.

I must also share that my largest financial loss, and most stressful time in business, was when I partnered in a retail store with someone who had plenty of expertise and little integrity—and I am being kind. This individual not only found creative ways to funnel profits to self-interests but started stores, under a different name, that sold a competing product in areas we already had locations. The two years I spent unraveling this mess was by far the most stressful time I have ever had in business. I joke now that I earned a master's degree in crises management.

TAKEAWAY:
Expertise in your industry is a pre-requisite for starting a successful business. If you don't have it, make sure to partner with, or hire, someone who does.

THOUGHTS TO CONSIDER:
1. Do you have the needed operational expertise in the industry you are going into?
2. If you do not have experience and knowledge in this industry, can you easily hire or partner with someone who does?

ACTION STEP:
List the areas of knowledge needed on one side of a piece of paper and on the other side, list who will bring these aspects to the business.

LEAD LIKE A COACH

When starting a business, you normally come to it having served as either an employee or a manager. Neither of these roles actually prepares you well to lead a business. Managing employees that receive their paycheck from someone other than you is not the same as managing when you are signing the checks. In the past, you probably never set the broad course for a company and only managed employees in ways your superiors had laid out for you. Or, as an employee, you never had a chance to lead at all.

Leadership is the X factor in starting and building a successful company. It will influence your entire development, from top to bottom. As a business owner, you have to chart the company's course. At the same time, especially in the beginning, you are at a disadvantage because you are probably not in a position to pay the highest wages. Furthermore, your talent as a leader may be average, at best.

I encourage you to think and lead as if you were a coach. Inspire, encourage, be firm when needed, and get the most out of the talent you have. Share your vision for the company from your first employee interview. You want to be a company they want to work for. If you can get employees excited and partnering with you in achieving success, then you have something special. Inspired employees create momentum, which is contagious, and customers will sense it.

A word of caution: If you find yourself regularly reminding employees that you own the company; you have lost the mantle of leadership. With work, you can reclaim that mantle, but it's best not to lose it in the first place. Take to heart the poignant words of Blaine Lee: "The great leaders are like the best conductors—they reach beyond the notes to reach the magic in the player."[35] Try to find—and activate—that magic in each person who works for you.

TAKEAWAY:
Lead like a coach.

THOUGHTS TO CONSIDER:
1. Think back to coaches, bandleaders and teachers that inspired you and what they said and did.
2. Buy a book on coaching and leadership and let it guide you to be the leader of your company.

ACTION STEP:
Write down three ways you can lead like a coach.

MAXIMIZE THE TALENT OF YOUR EMPLOYEES

To be a great leader you must be able to place people where they will be most productive. Here's another coaching analogy: Joe Gibbs, the Hall of Fame coach of the Washington Redskins, won three Super Bowl championships with three different quarterbacks, none of them destined for the Hall of Fame. How? Gibbs took these players and maximized their talent, so that they played like Hall of Famers. He did this by adopting strategies on the football field that played to their strengths.

Successful business owners will maximize the talent of their employees. It is your job to know what each person's talent is and to place him or her in a position to thrive. If you can tell someone is failing at something, over and over, you need to terminate or place the person in another area, and fast. I have heard leadership writer, John C. Maxwell make the claim, which I strongly agree with, that you are never going to take a weakness and make it a strength. On a scale of 1 to 10, you are never going to go from a 3 to an 8 or above, but you can take a 7 and get it to a 9 or 10. You do not want anyone performing below a 7 in anything for you.

4-star general Colin Powell puts his own spin on what he calls "situational leadership." He writes, "I adjust my style, within limits, to the strengths and weaknesses of my subordinates so that I understand what they can and can't do—compensating for weaknesses and taking advantage of their strengths."[36]

When interviewing, gather as much information as you can to assist you in placing people where they will succeed. For example: some people will never be able to talk to people, collect money or ask for the sale. In fact, not everybody knows how to talk to customers or to close a deal. Some people cannot handle confrontations of any kind. Probing these issues with prospective employees will help you identify strengths and weaknesses, and assign people accordingly. However, pay close attention to people in lower positions with talent that just need a "chance" to prove their value.

Remember, as your company grows, your employees should have the opportunity to grow, too. When they grow, the company grows even more.

TAKEAWAY:
Great leadership is placing people where they will excel.

THOUGHTS TO CONSIDER:
1. Can you think of things you have wanted to be good at but never excelled at, regardless of your effort?
2. What things just came easy to you from day one?

ACTION STEP:
When interviewing potential employees, ask questions to find their natural strengths.

BUILD AND TRUST YOUR "CABINET"

Movies and books on U.S. presidents always fascinate me. Who they appoint as cabinet members is instructive. The cabinet is the president's "go-to" team. All decisions will go through one or more of these individuals. I am disappointed when someone is appointed to a cabinet position just for political reasons and not because of his or her demonstrated talent and experience.

Your support team, which initially in most cases will be made up of non-employees, is crucial. It will usually consist of an accountant, lawyer, banker, and bookkeeper. Your accountant and lawyer will be used on an as-needed basis. In the very beginning, with all the software programs available, you or someone close to you may be able to handle the bookkeeping. If you plan to grow, at some point, you may need a professional bookkeeper. This is a small expense, as it requires a few hours a month and they charge a fraction of what an accountant costs. It is also good if you can get a bookkeeper that has worked with your accountant as this makes doing your taxes much easier. Bookkeepers will create your financial reports, which are important for you to review regularly.

Your support team can serve as your guardrails. Guardrails keep you safely on the road. A good accountant will let you know when you are moving into legal gray areas. I encourage you to let these individuals know you value their opinion and want to hear their feedback, because accountants can give you hard facts on the dollar value of your time, hiring decisions, and even what kind of vehicles to buy. If your company is a service provider, having a lawyer create your contracts is wise. I am not saying every contract, but your standard day-in, day-out service agreement should have a lawyer's review. I have a mediation agreement in all our contracts with our remodeling company. This alone has saved me a great deal of money, and I encourage you to ask your lawyer about it. A good banking relationship will help you grow your lines of credit, so have a banker you can speak to in person.

If you are going to have payroll, I cannot encourage you enough to use a payroll company. It can handle all employee taxes, social security, Medicare being withdrawn and paid timely. I have seen too many business owners get in trouble by not making timely employee tax payments. "In short," business writer, Jane Applegate, tells us, "Specialists are worth their salt because they know how to save you time and money."[37]

TAKEAWAY:
You will need a team of professionals around you to build a great company.

THOUGHTS TO CONSIDER:
1. Do you know anyone close to you who provides any of these services: bookkeeping, accounting, banking, or lawyer services?
2. Will you need a lawyer to help with any contracts or agreements for your business?

ACTION STEP:
Ask at least three other business owners for their recommendations for accounting, bookkeeping, banking, and legal matters. Form your professional cabinet.

GET TO KNOW YOUR LOCAL BANK

If you think you can present your business plan to your local bank and they will write you a check to get started, think again. If your bank gives you money, it will most likely be a secured loan. This means they will need collateral, such as your house, savings, or another asset.

Even if you don't get a secured loan, your local bank can be helpful in applying for a Small Business Loan (SBA). This is a government loan that, in most cases, helps existing businesses, but they have many different loan programs and you may be fortunate to find one that suits your needs.

Your bank will be an important team member in others ways, too. It can usually provide your business with Merchant Services, the ability to accept credit cards. I encourage you to shop around for the best rates. The bank can also provide no cost checking as well an overdraft protection program. If you have good credit, you may choose to get a business credit card that your bank can provide. As your business grows, your bank can provide you with financing to build, expand your office, or acquire fleet vehicles.

I have found small local regional banks to be the most likely to help my business needs. In fact, research shows that small banks are 3 times more likely than large institutions to issue loans to small businesses in their community.[38] At the same time, larger banks sometimes offer lower loan rates. Do your research. Some banks might provide incentives to keep a certain amount deposited—while others offer services to make the most of your profits. Other considerations might be whether the bank has a financial advisor to help you with investments and cash flow management, and whether it offers online banking services and readily available ATMs in your area.

TAKEAWAY:
Your bank may not give you start-up money, but they are an important part of your team.

THOUGHTS TO CONSIDER:
1. Do you presently have a bank that has been good to work with in regards to personal matters?
2. Ask other business owners what bank they would recommend. Do they work with a particular person at that bank?

ACTION STEP:
Open up a business account and begin a relationship with your new bank. This will be an important asset as your business grows.

DEVELOP A SUPPORT GROUP

We have all seen the value of support groups to help us get to the gym more regularly, lose weight, or meet other personal goals. The same is true in business. It's important to have one or more people in your life that can help you achieve your business dreams. We all need mentors and cheerleaders.

Your support group should consist of people who can encourage you, confront you, and at times, guide you. It is possible that one person can do it all, but more likely you will need a few people whose opinions you respect and listen to. As a general rule, I do not take advice from someone who has not accomplished what I am asking his or her advice about. For example, I do not take financial advice from someone who means well, but is broke.

A great organization from which to obtain business mentoring at no cost is SCORE, a nonprofit association dedicated to helping small businesses get off the ground, grow, and achieve their goals through education and mentorship. It is comprised almost entirely of retired businessmen, including former or active company CEOs. The group has been around over 50 years. You can apply for a local mentor at www.score.org.

In addition to a mentor, some business owners also seek out—and pay for—a business coach. A coach is someone who can work with you in a more hands-on way to develop badly needed leadership or management skills. Accepting the help of a coach can take great humility, but the personal and financial rewards are often well worth it.

Bob Nardelli, the former CEO of Home Depot has written: "I absolutely believe that people, unless coached, never reach their maximum capabilities."[39] Studies have documented extraordinary gains in leadership performance in companies in which the top executives are coached. Depending on your budget, and your possible shortfalls, you may want to explore this option, too.

TAKEAWAY:
It is helpful to have a support group.

THOUGHTS TO CONSIDER:
1. Who do you know that would be an encouraging member of your support group? This person does not need to have a business background.
2. Who do you know that has a wealth of proven business experience?

ACTION STEP:
Check out the SCORE association, and put in place your support group.

[6]

MARKETING IS NOT OPTIONAL

You may believe you have a great business idea, and that you're the right person to start this business. You may have even done all your planning, and assembled the best possible team. But if you don't find customers for your product or service, you unfortunately will not stay in business for long. Marketing is all about knowing who your ideal customer is, deciding what means of advertising will best reach this group with the message you have determined will make them use your product or service. The lessons in this section help you create your marketing plan, and think through specifics of your business name, website, taglines, and more. After completing the Action Steps in this section, you will walk away with a better plan for reaching the right customers and keep them coming back for more.

MARKETING IS MORE THAN A BUSINESS CARD

There are countless reasons why new businesses fail, but the two that I see repeating themselves are: starting with no competitive advantage and under-budgeting for marketing. Let's talk about the second one.

I meet and talk with business owners that sincerely think they have a marketing plan because they are in the phone book or just built a website. I also find it hysterical when I show up to my gym and see business cards posted en masse on a bulletin board. I know nothing else about these companies other than what their business cards say. This is not real marketing.

I also remember holding back laughter when I would be attempting to sell advertising space to a business owner in a run down office with no customer's in sight insisting, "I don't need any advertising, I am a word of mouth business."

I am a big fan of word-of-mouth, but it is rare that this can bring in enough customers to build a successful company. Digital media expert, Lisa Mooney explains why, "The limiting factor is that you, your staff and current customers will likely only reach out to those you come into contact with on a fairly regular basis. Over time, of course, these new contacts might use your service or buy your product and then spread the word to others, but this occurs over a long period. Your business might suffer from a small client base in the meantime."[40] You must spend enough money to reach your target market (ideal customer) with the reason (competitive advantage) they should buy your product/ service. That typically requires you to develop marketing messages adapted to different communications media—including print, online, and broadcast (radio and/or TV) outlets.

Nimble small business owners help sponsor and show up for important local events, including music festivals and fairs. They register with the Chamber of Commerce and go out of their way to become known in their community. Be pro-active and visible, not just hoping people will spread the word for you.

TAKEAWAY:

You must spend enough money to tell your ideal customer what your competitive advantages are through various marketing campaigns.

THOUGHTS TO CONSIDER:

1. How much of your net profit will you spend on advertising?
2. Do you see and hear a lot of advertising from your competition?

ACTION STEP:

Ensure that your marketing budget is enough to communicate your message to your ideal customer.

MARKETING 101

What do you need to communicate to a potential customer that would make them buy your product or service over your competition? This is the definition of marketing in the simplest way I can tell you. What would be the most cost effective ways to do this? Marketing is the your overall strategy. Advertising is the means. You will use various means of advertising to accomplish your marketing strategy.

Develop your marketing plan in 5 steps[41]:

1. The Lay of the Land: A.K.A. Competitive Intelligence and your Business Plan. Combine these in an honest and critical report on your business, your competition, and your customer base.
2. The Strategy: Define your product, your pricing strategy, and your sales goals for the year.
3. The Tactics: What is your detailed plan on how to meet your goals through each marketing avenue? Think advertising, sponsorship, events, and social media. This should not be short.
4. The Logistics: Where can you devote your marketing budget best over a specific period of time?
5. Report In: Write a 1-page summary of the above and insert it in your business plan.

Having a marketing plan will save you time and money. Advertising sales associates will be calling as soon as you open your doors for business. Tell them that you will "review their proposal and see how it fits within your marketing plan." They will take note of your preparedness, and will be less likely to try to over-sell you with "package deals" and other offers that you don't actually need.

A marketing plan will also allow you to carefully budget your advertising. For example: If you want to use radio to promote a new menu item, don't start with three radio stations. I would not even let a radio station sell me on its am station as an add-on, even though it might be a good deal. Why? Because I need to know if my initial placement worked. If I do all three stations, and I obtain lots of customers—or just a few—I will have no idea who deserves the credit, or the blame.

Note that it is perfectly okay to tweak your marketing plan, if you feel something is missing. That said, if one of your advertising initiatives doesn't work out as well you'd hoped, don't assume that your entire marketing plan is unsound. It could be a single media outlet—or maybe your timing wasn't the best. If advertising consistently fails to bring in business, though, you may need to revisit your assumptions.

TAKEAWAY:
Think big picture: Have a marketing plan, not single event advertising.

THOUGHTS TO CONSIDER:
1. Have you ever been involved in marketing decision before?
2. Can you think of a marketing message that reached you?

ACTION STEP:
Develop a one-year marketing plan. If this exercise seems overwhelming I will help you in a later lesson in this chapter. (Warning: avoid annual contracts in regards to advertising if at all possible)

ADVERTISING 101

You may remember Cliffs Notes from when you were in school. Cliffs Notes took a book you usually did not have the time or desire to read and condensed it just enough so that you could pass a test. This is what I'm going to do now.

Advertising is the primary way to reach potential customers with your message. The desired outcome of advertising is for customers to use your company. TV, radio, direct mail, and websites are all venues for business advertising.

What methods of advertising will work best for you? TV is usually the most expensive but allows you to show your product/service in action. Radio allows you to best tell a story. Radio and TV both allow you to use testimonies. Direct mail is good for coupons or limited offers and events.

Website marketing is the new phone book—you must have a presence. Your local newspaper, if it has good readership, promotes events well. Tradeshows can also have tremendous value if you are not there with ten of your competitors. Local community events are also potentially effective.

I am a strong believer in exclusivity. Try always to be the only company in any direct mail, print media, or event that does what your company does or offers. I do not always achieve this, but I am shocked at how often I actually do. It's all about staying ahead of the competition. Put another way: Try to find a competitive advantage to market to your ideal customer.

TAKEAWAY:

Understanding all the means of advertising will save you money as you can better determine what will serve your company the best.

THOUGHTS TO CONSIDER:

1. What means of advertising will help you reach your ideal customer?
2. If you can only use one, which method of advertising is best for your business?

ACTION STEP:

Get pricing on all the advertising techniques you may need to reach your ideal customer.

WHO IS YOUR IDEAL CUSTOMER?

Who are going to be your customers? No, the answer is probably not "every-one." Who will most have the need for your service/product? Will it be women or men? What about age groups: teenagers, those ages 18-24, 35-49, or older? Do you know? Ideally, yes.

These are your "demographics," the population sub-groups that are most likely to use your company. The more specific your demographics, the more effective your marketing will be, and also less expensive, as you will not be marketing to those not likely to use your product or service.

Trade associations are a good source for finding this information. Another source is to call someone who is doing your business in another city like yours. Surprisingly, most people are happy to brag about what works for them. Again, business guru, Rhonda Abrams has some advice on how to be pro-active, "You should absolutely try to capture the names and contact information of everyone who comes to your website or place of business or who connects with you on social media. After all, they've sought you out, so they're prime prospects."[42] Your website designer or web host may help you to do this data collection.

If you are starting a service company, try calling a local business that you have personally used. If your business in no way competes with theirs, they will, in most cases, be happy to share with you what has worked for them.

Demographics are not static. You may find that you have a core customer base but as you introduce new types of products, or find ways to target other demographic segments, you can expand your base. However, never forget who your core customer base is, and make sure that you keep this base happy.

TAKEAWAY:
You must determine your ideal customer.

THOUGHTS TO CONSIDER:
1. Who will buy your product or use your service?
2. Can you see why determining your ideal customer will save you money?

ACTION STEP:
Determine who is most likely to use your service or product.

WHAT'S IN A NAME? A LOT.

The naming of your business is more important than you might think. It should be viewed as a significant step in starting a successful business. Entrepreneur magazine notes: "The right name can make your company the talk of the town. The wrong one can doom it to obscurity and failure."[43]

I believe you shouldn't try to be too cute or creative with your name. Businesses that are entirely web-based can use odd names such as Google, Bing, Go-Daddy, etc. They are seeking uniqueness and something easy to remember—and search. However, a non-Internet business should have a name that clearly tells the customer what kind of business you are, and the type of service you're providing.

I see too many businesses with names that give no hint as to what they do. This makes marketing tough and more expensive, as you first need to educate the consumer on what your business is offering. A good friend of mine who owns a sign company once designed a sign for a business named Green Leaf. From name alone, you don't know the nature of their business. Is it a restaurant? Is it a health food store? It helps to choose a name that is easy to remember and not too long.

If your business serves a particular geographic location, consider putting that area in the business name. For instance, Central Virginia Moving would be an appropriate name if that were the location I service. Then again, if you plan to have multiple locations in the future, don't choose a name with a limited geographic scope. For example, Panera Bread started as the St. Louis Bread Company, but as they began to franchise, the original name no longer applied. A new name required new logos, new signs, and a new branding strategy. Even after the name officially changed to "Panera" for all the establishments in the U.S., customers in St. Louis demanded that the original stores go back to the old name. This meant completely different set of signs and promotional materials for one city than in the rest of the country.

TAKEAWAY:

Your business name should clearly communicate what your business does.

THOUGHTS TO CONSIDER:

1. Do you plan at some point to be in other locations or servicing a larger area?
2. Does your name clearly communicate what you provide?

ACTION STEP:

Come up with a list of at least five possible names for your business. Before finalizing any name, do a domain name search and check with your state corporation commission to see if the name is available.

ELEVATOR PITCH

This is a drill down on your (USP) Unique Sales Proposition from chapter 2. What is it that your company offers (product or service) and why should customer's choose you over your competition? You need to be able to own some simple statements that communicate this in a way that makes prospective customer's want to know more about your company.

This message should solve a problem that your ideal customer has. If you are an accounting firm what is the number one problem you can solve for your customers? "We guarantee the largest tax return allowed by law in the shortest amount of time possible." The fact is if you do you job correctly both these items should happen. What sounds better Smith Accounting or Maximum Tax Solutions? Nobody does a better job of communicating how to pick a name, logo or core message better then Jan Jantsch in his book Duct Tape Marketing. On a personal note I feel like marketing is my strength yet I read this book twice and took notes like a first year freshman.

Now that you have an idea of how to create a core marketing message, which is Jan's term for Unique Selling Proposition, you need to be able to communicate this in a quick phrase that could possibly be your elevator pitch. An elevator pitch is what you do for a living and makes you or your company different. This should be catchy and bring out a key area of differentiation from your competitors.

Using the accounting example from above your elevator pitch may be " I help my clients pay the least amount of taxes possible by law." This will surely have the person wanting to know more.

TAKEAWAY:

Elevator Pitch is a short catchy phrase of what your company does and makes you different.

THOUGHTS TO CONSIDER:

1. What are 2-3 problems your company can solve?
2. What problems do you think you can solve better or faster then your competition?

ACTION STEP:

Write an elevator pitch you and your employees will commit to memory.

DEVELOP AN IMAGE

Once you have a name, the next step is to create a brand image through your logo and color schemes. These items need to be carefully thought out on the front end. In Stephen Covey's book, *7 Habits of Highly Effective People*, he introduces the concept of "begin with the end in mind." This principle is a must for anyone starting a business. If you hope to own a successful business, it needs to look like one from day one.

In regards to color schemes, keep it simple, with no more than two colors. More than two and it gets more expensive when purchasing a sign and uniforms. It's also hard to work with when doing print media. Logos should be simple and professional. The web is loaded with companies that can assist you with your logo. Your web designer may also be helpful in this area. Your goal, with your logo and color scheme, is to create a professional image.

Consider these 5 points for an effective logo[44]:

- Timelessness: Don't date your business for this moment in time. Think long term for a logo, just like you would for the business: clean and classic.
- Adaptability: Your logo should look good on a t-shirt, a flyer, and a business card. That is to say, your logo printed big, medium, and small shouldn't compromise the image and works in any context.
- Unique: Without going out on a limb, distinguish your logo from all others in the industry. Take multiple ideas from different sources and merge the best qualities into one dynamite logo. Think the Starbucks mermaid and McDonald's golden arches.
- Appropriate: Don't reinvent the wheel. Your potential market is used to a certain style. Balance what customers expect with what makes your company different from the rest.

- Less is More: Stick with one font, and never use more than two colors. Simplicity is memorable and pleasing to the eye. This also makes it easier to use the same logo on t-shirts, cards, etc.

Not to complicate things, but once you have a logo and color scheme, you may want a tagline that is a slogan tied to your logo. Some examples: *Subway: Eat Fresh* or Nike's famous *Just Do It*.

TAKEAWAY:
You need a professional image.

THOUGHTS TO CONSIDER:
1. What logos can you easily identify with companies?
2. What taglines do you associate with companies?

ACTION STEP:
Finalize a logo, with color scheme, and possibly a tagline.

YES, YOU NEED A WEBSITE

Many would-be small business owners wonder whether they need an online presence. If they are doing all of their business locally, they figure that traditional advertising should be enough. Moreover, if none of their products or services will ever be sold online, they see even less reason to invest in a web site.

This is archaic thinking. Once upon a time, a web site seemed like a flashy "extra" that only trendy companies on the cutting edge of media communications needed. Today, however, a web site is an integral part of business marketing and advertising. Most of your prospective customers, even those born during the heyday of radio and television, are surfing the Internet. Developing an online presence is as essential as having a business card.

Websites can vary greatly in sophistication and cost. At a minimum you need a "homepage" that functions like a business "storefront." Prospective customers should be able to find your products and services described there, as well as basic contact information. Some companies offer a deeper "window" into their operations by posting their mission and vision statements, plus an open letter from the owner and photographs of the store and company staff.

One of the beauties of websites is that you can start small, and build as you grow. You may find that some competitors still don't have web sites—all the more reason for you to have one. Once you have your site, with a distinct domain name, and URL, make sure it's listed on all your communications.

You can hire a website designer to help you develop an attractive site that fits your budget and marketing/advertising needs. Designers can help you choose titles and keywords that will raise your visibility on search engines like Google. You can also pay Google directly to achieve higher visibility.

There are also a growing number of DIY (Do It Yourself) systems like WordPress that allow you to design your own website. These systems are cheaper, have built-in templates, and have the added advantage that you won't need someone else to manage the site. You can add fresh content as needed, at no extra cost.

A web site is enormously cost effective (about $10 a month) while the prices of other forms of advertising, including radio and print, have shot through the roof. In addition, studies have shown that more people search online these days than consult the yellow pages.

TAKEAWAY:
Developing an online presence is a cost-effective way to expand your marketing and advertising.

THOUGHTS TO CONSIDER:
1. Do you have the ability to build a professional grade website on your own?
2. When you look for products and services, do you search for them on the Internet?

ACTION STEP:
Review the websites of your prospective competitors, and research website development

ESTABLISH YOUR REPUTATION

When starting a business, you may think you don't have a reputation yet, but in the Internet age, your reputation can become known on day one. With the popularity of Angie's List (www.angieslist.com) and Reputation.com, how your customers view your company has become big business. Before you open your doors to the public it would be wise to provide your service or product to as many people as you know and have them provide feedback on sites such as Angie's List, Yahoo, Yelp, and other user reviewer sites. Also have them provide testimonials on your website.

In an age when people are using the web and smartphones to look up businesses and make quick decisions, this is a critical field to master. According to a Harvard Business School report, "a one-star increase on Yelp can lead to a 9% increase in sales," and "Four out of five consumers, or 80%, reverse their purchase decisions based on negative online reviews" according to an Online Influence Trend Tracker survey.[45]

You need to be aware of what people are saying about you on a regular basis. Sign up for Google Alerts to know when your business name is mentioned online. You may even consider spending some cash to enlist the service of companies like ReviewTrakers, Netvibes, Reputation.com, or Trakur. They can send you alerts and provide support in managing your online reputation ranging from $19 a month to $5,000 and up, a year (for large businesses with bad reps). But, if you see something negative on the Internet, contact the customer who wrote it and make it right. Do this privately and respectfully. When you have made it right, ask them to revise their comments. You may win a repeat customer too.

One of the best ways possible to be viewed positively by customers who have yet to use your company is to be a member of the Better Business Bureau. This organization carries tremendous credibility and membership is only a few hundred dollars. If you only did one thing, joining the BBB and meeting their customer satisfaction commitments would be a good strategy. Another strategy for having a good reputation is being a member of credible industry associations.

TAKEAWAY:

You must be aware of your reputation, and do everything you can to make it positive.

THOUGHTS TO CONSIDER:

1. What is the reputation you want? (Quality, dependability, etc.)
2. How can your business provide this repeatedly?

ACTION STEP:

Have friends and associates try your business products or services and share their experiences via the Internet or testimonials on your site.

JOIN BUSINESS ASSOCIATIONS

A simple way to build credibility and to learn more about your industry is to join associations. These are also a great way to learn what is working for others within your industry. They may also offer discounts on products and professional services you may need.

Associations usually have a logo/seal that can be used to show your affiliation, which is a good marketing bonus. Using these association logos in your advertising gives credibility. The more support you have when starting a business, the better, so being a part of an association offers no downsides.

Talk to other business owners in your area and industry. Find out what associations they are actively involved in. Ask which associations they find worthwhile and why.

General associations like the Chamber of Commerce may be good for networking and sharing local marketing tips. However, Industry-specific associations might help with labor recruitment, training, getting involved in lobbying and keeping up on changes to regulations and other important industry news.

Additionally, associations can provide a social network of like-minded people with similar experiences. As a boss and manager of employees, you may feel isolated—especially when you are just getting started. Keith Ashmus, the chairman of the National Small Business Association explains, "[Business owners] often can't talk to their employees about what concerns them and they need to talk to a peer who is not a competitor.... An association is a great way to find those connections."[46]

TAKEAWAY:
Industry associations offer many advantages.

THOUGHTS TO CONSIDER:
1. Which association is most credible in your industry? Often it will be the oldest and/or has the most members.
2. Which association offers the most benefits that you are most in need of?

ACTION STEP:
After you have determined which are the best associations for your company, join at least one of them. Include their logo on your website and print media.

SYSTEMATICALLY SURVEY CUSTOMERS

Customer feedback is crucial to being a successful company. How well your product and service meet the expectations of the people buying it will determine whether they are repeat customers, or speak positively to others about your company. "When surveying, it is important to remember that you are measuring customers' perceptions and not necessarily reality," warns the National Business Research Institute.[47] "Customer perceptions are more important than reality. This is counterintuitive but true nonetheless."

You need to be a collector of customer feedback from day one. Start your business with a customer survey in place. This should be simple, but needs to ask a few key questions:

1. Did the product/service meet your expectations?
2. Would you use our company or buy our product again?
3. Would you refer our product or service to a friend? Why or why not?
4. Do you have a specific concern that needs to be addressed?

Customer surveys can be used in advertising to great effectiveness. I began collecting surveys from day one with a service company I started. The first year, I had a staff person call every customer and ask the above four questions. A year later, we created a postcard that we mailed with a thank you letter to every customer we served.

Today, we have surveyed over 10,000 customers, with 99% responding positively. We also advertise this fact: "With over 10,000 customers formally surveyed, 99% said they would use us again and refer us to a friend." We can also use the survey to pick up new quotes for customer testimonials with the permission of the customer. These facts and quotes give the customer great confidence when choosing our company. We have carried this same plan over to our property managements and property development companies. Clients and customers want you to value their feedback.

TAKEAWAY:

Have a systematic process in place to receive customer feedback from day one.

THOUGHTS TO CONSIDER:

1. Are there one or two additional questions you would add to your survey that are specifically tailored to your business?
2. What would be the most effective method for you to receive this feedback?

ACTION STEP:

Create a customer survey and determine your process for how you are going to use it in your marketing.

DEVELOP CUSTOMER TESTIMONIES

I am a big fan of testimonial advertising. This is when a customer shares his or her personal experience with your product or service. Prospective customers are not surprised when you, as the owner, brag about how great your business is. They kind of expect it. But when customers share their experience, it is powerful.

New business owners tend to believe they need to be in business a long period of time before they have testimonies, let alone advertise them. This is not true. Gather these testimonies even before you open your doors. These pre-launch testimonies might serve as Research and Development (R&D), pointing out some flaw or giving you a new idea. Have family, friends, and colleagues experience your product or service and write compelling testimonies. Your website should feature such testimonies from day one.

Collecting testimonies after you are in business requires some legwork. But, marketing blogger, Kristi Hines, has ideas on how to get customer testimonials to get you started in the right direction.[48]

1. Facebook Reviews: This is built into a business formatted Facebook page. Cut and paste.
2. LinkedIn Reviews: Businesses can't have references posted, but individuals (you and staff) can.
3. YouTube Video Reviews: With no money, you can post videos on YouTube and embed them in your website. This puts a human face on the review, making it that much stronger.
4. Local Search Directories: Reviews on Google Places, Yelp, and Yahoo will pop up when customers search for businesses like yours.

The method of communicating testimonies is up to you, based on your advertiser demographics and costs. I personally have found radio to be the most effective means of communicating a testimony. Radio commercials are typically 60 seconds while

TV commercials are most likely 15 or 30 seconds. Some viewers are now recording TV programs and fast forwarding through the commercials. The advantage of TV, though, is that it allows for "before and after" visual imagery.

TAKEAWAY:
Before you open your business, and from every day you are in business, gather testimonies like a boy collecting baseball cards.

THOUGHTS TO CONSIDER:
1. What competitive advantage do you want your customers to communicate in their testimony?
2. Can you think of at least ten people who can experience your company and offer a testimony before you open for business?

ACTION STEP:
Have five to ten testimonies on your website from day one.

LOOK FOR ADDED VALUE

Can your product perform more functions than the competition? Do you offer additional complimentary services? Consider how you might bring additional value to your customers. A fresh competitive advantage might also allow you to increase your prices.

I recently was shopping for a vacuum and found one model that also had a hand-sized vacuum built inside the larger vacuum. It was amazing to me. I saw that I was actually getting two vacuums in one. The product was higher in price but it clearly offered more value, too. I did not hesitate to purchase it.

Another example is a car wash I frequent. My car generates a great deal of brake dust on the wheels. It drives me crazy. (It is even more ridiculous that this high-end German automaker, which I will not mention directly for fear of being sued, has not figured out how to solve this issue, but that is another subject). Before you enter the automatic wash area, there is a bucket-and-brush that allows you to pre-clean your wheels. This is the only way I can get my wheels to look truly amazing. I drive out of my way to use this car wash because it offers something as simple as a self-serve bucket with a brush.

CEO of RecruitLoop.com, Michael Overell writes, "In order to add value, you need to know your clients intimately; what their business goals are, what their needs are and what their strengths and weaknesses are. By identifying these things, you will also identify the areas where you can offer added value to them."[49] Once you understand your clients, you can maximize the added value by offering additional services, resources, attention, or expertise. You may also consider strengthening the relationship by becoming a customer of your client's business.

Look for ways to create "added-value" for your product or service. It may be something simple or small that sets you apart and allows you to add additional profit.

Try to think broadly in terms of its branding or competitive advantage potential. If customers consistently say, "Oh yeah, that's the company that offers that special extra," you are on your way to something exciting. Once you have determined how you will add value, communicate it in your marketing.

TAKEAWAY:
Provide more value than your competition.

THOUGHTS TO CONSIDER:
1. Can you think of a recent purchase you made because you felt like you were getting additional value for your money?
2. What additional value can you provide at minimal cost?

ACTION STEP:
Identify where you can offer more value than your competition, and ensure this is a component of your marketing strategy.

START BRANDING EARLY

Branding is a promise you make to your customers about an important quality or attribute they can expect to receive from using your product or service. Take a word of phrase that summarizes this promised quality and start to use it in your marketing materials. In your advertising, repeat it over and over again, or find a way to consistently represent it visually.

Branding can be very effective. For example, when you think of "safety" in regards to an automobile, you probably think of Volvo. The company has spent decades branding that attribute in relation to its product.

A brand is often closely related to other company attributes, such as a logo, trademark, or slogan Nike's "Just Do It" slogan was a core part of the company's brand at one time. It associated Nike with a lifestyle attitude. It's so popular that people used it in everyday conversation. U.S. Army uses Army Strong, which implies strength at a different level.

The truth is a good brand isn't built overnight, simply by proclaiming it. Entrepreneur, Stelios Haji-Ioannou notes: "Your brand is created out of customer contact and the experience your customers have of you."[50] There's no need to wait to start thinking about how to brand your company. Start experimenting in your earliest advertising messages.

Try to be original. Do not copy any existing branding words or phrases. Here are some qualities you might want to brand: durable, low prices, locally made or grown, handcrafted, fast, convenient, or professional. These are just a few, and they often can be drawn from your company's competitive advantages. You may want to pick a theme that you want to brand for the next year or two.

I have recently been branding the phrase "The Advantage Difference." I have a radio personality introduce me by saying they have used our services personally, and they ask me as the owner, what I think makes our company different. I then begin with one of our differences. I have a list of six that I believe separates us from our competitors. This is just one of the countless ideas you can brand.

TAKEAWAY:
Make a commitment to branding one or more of your competitive advantages.

THOUGHTS TO CONSIDER:
1. What companies do you associate with a word or short phrase?
2. What words best describe what you want your company to be identified with?

ACTION STEP:
List your competitive advantages and circle phrases that would be good for branding. Choose one word or phrase you will begin to brand your company with.

PROMOTE "WORD OF MOUTH"

I remember for years hearing about how great Apple computers were. The problem was their products seemed to be consistently higher in price. Therefore, I always bought the standard PC. Eventually, my son wore me down, and I bought an Apple. Guess what? It's worth every penny.

I am not a computer guy, but one touch of Apple's keyboard told me it was a superior product. Its lightweight monitor was another huge selling point. I have since told everyone how much I love Apple computers.

That's what's known as "word of mouth." As your brand grows, customer word of mouth becomes more important. Create a product or service that people want to tell others about. It will become advertising that you won't have to pay for. Do all you can to create the perfect experience for your customers, so they will tell everyone they know.

You can also try to cultivate some key "influentials" early on. This is why you have to be a people person. The successful speaker, entrepreneur, and author, Rhonda Abrams, gives this advice, "Try to capture the contact information of those you meet at business or social events and trade shows. They're all leads—potential customers or referral services."[51] These are people who, by virtue of their position in a community, naturally tend to speak to lots of other people and whose opinions may be highly valued. If they are familiar with your pricing and product, and are sold on your company, they can spread the word "virally"—perhaps through a blog, Facebook, or another community-based information network.

TAKEAWAY:
You want customers to brag to everyone about your product or service.

THOUGHTS TO CONSIDER:
1. Can you remember a buying experience you had that you told everyone about?
2. What was it that impressed you so much?

ACTION STEP:
Commit to having a product/service that is so outstanding that customers will want to brag about your company to everyone they know.

DEVELOP A START-UP STORY

Think about how Sam Walton founded Wal-Mart in a small town in Arkansas based on low prices and revolutionary thinking about how to organize a new kind of general store. Or, how Steve Jobs saw a demonstration of Xerox's $300 computer mouse and went home to make a prototype using a ping-pong ball resulting in a $15 product. And did you know that the first Nike shoe was hand-made in a garage using a waffle iron to form the shoe treads? People, especially Americans, love stories of humble beginnings and creative vision. You may or may not fit this mold, but I bet you have a story to tell.

One way to get your business started on the right foot is with some sort of press release. Newspapers are always looking for content and "feel good" stories. Local radio stations also seek content and are a good source for a five-minute interview with a local talk station host. A simple article or interview that tells about you and your business idea is powerful. These press releases also are valuable content for your website.

People like to support causes and after reading/hearing about your business, they may give you a try. I added a construction division years ago and used a story in the paper to launch it. The amount of calls we received was simply incredible. I basically created my own "infomercial" by purchasing a one-page ad, and then filled it with the story of how I came to start my company—and why. I have since used this press release method on every company from retail to property management.

Use your start-up story to introduce yourself and your vision, and to explain what will be unique about your company. Your story should be something you use for years when hiring or selling your company's product/service.

What I love most about the Olympics is the short biographies of the athletes. These stories are used to get people to watch because they now have someone to cheer for. Get people to cheer for the success of your business.

TAKEAWAY:
Press releases can be a valuable first line of advertising.

THOUGHTS TO CONSIDER:
1. What about your company or yourself is interesting and would make a good story?
2. Struggling for ideas? A surefire winner is to explain how many jobs you hope to create.

ACTION STEP:
Contact your local media and create a press release.

YOUR 1ST MARKETING PLAN

If we were honest, most of us would admit that we couldn't have learned how to ride a bicycle without the use of training wheels. Yes, I'm talking about those goofy small wheels that sat just outside our back tires, which allowed our bicycle to keep from toppling over. Training wheels allowed us to gain confidence.

Let me be your training wheels, in regards to developing your first marketing plan. I am going to illustrate using a property management company I own.

1. *Who is my ideal customer?* Those who own rental property and need to rent it. This is usually someone older, with higher incomes.
2. *What is the most cost-effective way to reach this ideal customer?* In short, what means of advertising will reach the most ideal customers for the least amount of money? For us, the answers are:

- Morning radio 6am-10am on our adult contemporary station
- Evening news on our most watched local TV station
- The Sunday newspaper

3. *What message can I communicate to convert this ideal customer into a paying customer?* This will usually come from your competitive advantages, a quality you seek to brand, or an added value you hope to provide. The message we advertise is: We will try to rent your home with urgency, knowing that a vacant property is a failure on our part. We have a radio ad that asks, "Are you losing money each month as your property sits empty?" This, we have determined, is the biggest fear property owners have. They need to get their property rented. We seek to meet that need, and through our marketing, we establish an emotion to convey that we understand that need. We have a voice that conveys this emotion in our radio commercial.

The amount of money you have to budget for marketing will dictate whether you have a secondary campaign, perhaps featuring a TV commercial or another means to best reach your ideal customer.

TAKEAWAY:
Your company must have a detailed plan to reach your customers.

THOUGHTS TO CONSIDER:
1. Can you see where this can be fun, thinking of strategic ways to reach your ideal customer in the most affordable way?
2. Is this whole exercise like learning a foreign language? If it is, contact a local advertising agency and have them develop a marketing strategy for your company.

ACTION STEP:
Create a detailed marketing plan.

SALES PROCESS IN THREE STEPS

Assuming you have a product or service that you have been able to market well, you now must make the sale. The sale is when currency changes hands, and without it you have no business.

Nothing is more important than the ability to sell the product. How often have you seen a ridiculous product advertised that you doubt actually works but is still selling briskly? The company that produced it has mastered the sales process, because the company was built from the ground up with one goal in mind: to *sell* the product. You have to do the same and sell, sell, sell. "If it doesn't sell, it isn't creative," according to Ad executive David Ogilvy.

Step one is to communicate to a potential customer that your product/service fills a need/desire. Step two is to give confidence that you can provide what the customer is seeking. Sales expert and speaker, Mark Hunter says this another way, "Regardless of what I'm selling, what the customer is buying first is me."[52] Testimonies are helpful in step two. Step three is offering customers a "no-risk" offer. If they don't like the product, they can return it, and you will refund their money. This offer can remove an important last hurdle to purchase. In a service business, your step 3 would be returning payment if the customer were not satisfied.

Publisher and journalist, William Feather has a great maxim on how salesmanship doesn't stop after money the changes hands: "Once you have sold a customer, make sure he is satisfied with your goods. Stay with him until the goods are used up or worn out. Your product may be of such long life that you will never sell him again, but he will sell you and your product to his friends."[53]

TAKEAWAY:

Do these three things well and you can sell your product or service:

1. Fulfill a need/desire.
2. Establish confidence and trust in your product/service.
3. Reduce customer risk with a warranty and a simple no hassle return policy.

THOUGHTS TO CONSIDER:

1. How will you build confidence in your product/service?
2. What warranty will you offer that will reduce risk and buyer's anxiety?

ACTION STEP:

Survey a few friends with your sales pitch and ask if you met all three criteria for a sale.

[7]

KNOW YOUR NUMBERS

Starting a business requires a lot of attention to numbers. You may be using your own money to invest in starting your business. You may rely on loans and credit from others. Regardless, to be profitable, you need to think critically about your operating costs, pricing structure, and how much you require to meet your own personal expenses. This section contains lessons about managing and protecting your bottom line.

KNOW YOUR OPERATING COSTS

Lack of capital is the number one reason businesses fail. Though, I would argue, if you had a qualified business idea to start with, you might not have needed so much money. Regardless, you need to determine how much capital is required to operate your business.

Determine all costs associated with operating your business: rent, utilities, labor, advertising, contractors, supplies, website, loan payments, inventory, etc. This should be an exhaustive summary of what it takes financially to keep your business up and running. You can trim or expand this list later. As a preliminary exercise, though, make sure you list every possible operating expense, including any debt repayments. Here is a sample list to get you started:

- Rent
- Office expenses
- Utilities
- Travel and vehicle expenses
- Advertising
- Insurance
- Salary and wages
- Maintenance and repairs, such as trash removal, janitorial service, and lawn care
- Inventory
- Taxes
- Debt
- Professional fees

From your list, you will establish your standard operating budget. How much start-up capital you need is determined, in part, by this budget. The other factor is how much average revenue you can generate.

The baseline cost of operating your company is a figure that you will monitor for the life of the business. If the figure rises, then your income better rise with it.

TAKEAWAY:
You need to know what it will cost to operate your business.

THOUGHTS TO CONSIDER:
1. What expenses are absolutely critical for you to open your doors?
2. After establishing your costs, see if there is anything that can be removed? Is there any expense that can be lowered by negotiating a better price or better terms?

ACTION STEP:
Create a list of all your business expenses. Make it as detailed as possible. Then use this list to determine how much operating capital you will need.

RESERVES

There is a new television show that is starting to grow on me. It's called "Doomsday Preppers." It features individuals and families that are committed to thinking through and planning for every conceivable disaster scenario. They build a bunker that can withstand a nuclear blast and stockpile enough food, water, and medicine to survive.

It may sound counter-intuitive, but one of the best ways to build your business is to try to insulate it against the threat of destruction. CEO and venture capitalist, Cindy Padnos recommends raising enough startup money to last you for one business quarter: "Yes, you should be as capital-efficient as possible, but you also need enough money to ensure your survival if everything doesn't go as planned—because it never does."[54] From day one, you should begin to establish a cash and credit "stockpile." Essentially, the stockpile is a "strategic" or "prudent" reserve of cash and non-cash assets that you never actually tap to run the business day to day.

The reserve is there in the event of an emergency. It can be large or small at the outset, but it should be equal to your operating expenses for a projected period of interruption in which your business may be unable to generate new income.

If nothing came in for 60 days, how long could you keep your doors open? That is one preliminary way to estimate the size of your stockpile or reserve. The size of the reserve can and should grow over time, in part because the size and value of your business is growing, and therefore, the costs associated with a loss of business income are growing, too.

You also need to grow un-used lines of credit (LOC's). Many businesses don't focus on developing new credit lines until it is already too late. If you're managing a financially stable business with no existing line of credit, stop by to see your local bank and ask what you need to do to establish a line. Also, get to know the bank manager on a friendly personal basis. During credit crunches, the bank will have to make tough decisions about who to lend to. Increase your chances that your business is on the banks' priority list.

TAKEAWAY:
Be optimistic about your business but still plan for worst-case scenarios. Start now to grow your cash and credit reserves to survive any possible disruption to your operations.

THOUGHTS TO CONSIDER:
1. Can you think of things that could occur that would threaten the future of your business?
2. Can you think of a business that is no longer around that experienced events that they could not withstand?

ACTION STEP:
Begin on day one building a cash and credit reserve.

CREDIT IS YOUR LIFEBLOOD

Credit is the lifeblood of your business, as it keeps all the vital organs of your business functioning. Get credit, then get more credit, and when you are done getting that credit, get a touch more. The Small Business Network advises "the best time to apply for a credit line is when you don't need it. Lenders are most likely to grant a LOC when your business' cash flow is strong and your balance sheet is clean."[55]

If you are averse to debt, good luck owning a business. I am not a fan of debt, but you need it to operate your business. For example, I have a good friend who owns a sign company. A new crane costs $250K. Few small businesses can afford that kind of capital expense without obtaining a loan to help pay for it.

If you are giving customers 30 days to pay their invoices, you will need credit to operate while waiting for these payments. The basic credit you need to seek is overdraft protection on checking accounts. This can come in handy if a large check written by a customer is returned, as well as a payment you are waiting to receive does not arrive.

Overdraft credit usually has the highest interest rate and should only be used in an emergency. You may also get a line of credit from your bank, which is very common for established businesses, and even new businesses where the owner has personal assets to secure the loan. These credit lines usually range from $25K and up.

A word of caution with lines of credit: They can be called in each year by the lender. This means at the end of the term, which is usually one year, they can ask you to pay the outstanding balance in full. They also do not have to renew the loan. I have had banks call this loan in, and it creates a panic. They will also request your financial statement at the end of each year and decide if they want to continue this line of credit.

It never hurts to have a few credit cards hidden in your desk drawer for emergencies. Be very careful using business credit cards, as you can easily abuse them. I've had an experience where a monthly credit card statement came, and no one in the business could adequately explain what the charges were for.

TAKEAWAY:
Get as much credit as you can.

THOUGHTS TO CONSIDER:
1. Have you handled credit in your personal finances well? How you have handled credit in your personal life will usually correlate with how you will handle them in business.
2. Will your business require large capital expenses that you will need to finance?

ACTION STEP:
Acquire as much credit as you can and commit to using it sparingly.

TAKE A MODEST SALARY

You may get rich starting your own business. I am confident that if you have the right business idea and run your business correctly, it will happen. The problem is that new business owners tend to pay themselves too much salary initially when their start-up money is coming from someone else.

As an entrepreneur, yes, you stand to lose a lot of time and money. But you also can reap the rewards in a big way, too. So don't get into the mindset of what is "fair" to pay yourself for the long hours and stress. Your employees are not in the same boat as you. That's why you will pay your employees wages based on what their time, labor, effort, and accomplishments are worth to the business. If you got paid in the same way, you would bleed the business dry in no time.

So the simplest answer, according to Chicago entrepreneur, Jay Goltz, is this: "I think business owners should pay themselves whatever is left—whatever is left, that is, after everyone and everything else has been paid and after money for growth and paying down debt has been factored in."[56] But not every business owner can afford to earn nothing the first months after a launch.

I have a missionary's mindset about salary. Take just the bare minimum you need to survive. Prior to starting, you may find it helpful to see which loans may have a deferral program for hardship. Usually they include auto loans, student loans, and even mortgages. I have found that you can defer most loans two months.

The SBA offers some commonsensical advice on this issue: "If you are still in startup mode and have no profit history or aren't turning a profit yet, you might want to set your salary by reviewing your own personal costs. What do you need to support your modest, startup lifestyle? Defer everything above and beyond that."[57]

Remember, cash is your oxygen. Don't be the one who takes it all.

TAKEAWAY:

In the start-up phase of your business, your pay should be only enough to survive.

THOUGHTS TO CONSIDER:
1. How much were you planning to pay yourself in the first year?
2. Could this amount be lower? What expenses in your life are not priorities?

ACTION STEP:

Contact all your loan providers and see what deferral programs are available.

AVOID UNNECESSARY EXPENSES

I am not a big fan of starting a company without having some of your own money at risk. I think it helps to have a little "skin in the game." As I suspect that you'll manage your own money better than money from an outside source.

In the beginning, you have your startup capital, but little to no income. The funds you start with should be for employee salaries and overhead, until you start turning a profit. And the rate you draw down on those funds before breaking even is called the "burn rate." Judge your burn rate, like a pilot judges a runway during take off. When you've run out of cash, you've run out of runway.

Veteran startup mentor, Martin Zwilling likes this image of the runway. His advice is simple but can prevent a disaster: "As a rule, you need to review your burn rate every month, and manage it every day. The components are simple—expenses and income. If you don't have any income, the job is even simpler, be ruthless about controlling expenses. Think twice, at least, before committing to any big outlays, and add up small ones."[58] He also suggests raising more money than needed before launch, paying investors with equity and a percentage of future revenue, and using bartering to reduce costs.

To add any unneeded expenses while still in start-up mode is just plain foolish. Recently, I was eating at a new restaurant, and while speaking with an employee, he shared that all employees receive gym memberships. This is a great perk for employees, but should only be implemented AFTER a company has become profitable.

It turns out that the restaurant we were eating at went out of business shortly thereafter. Like so many restaurants, unstable business and a failure to control operating costs killed the enterprise. The parents of the owner had put their house up as security for his initial loan. Needless to say, they ended up losing their house also.

Always think lean. Subject every prospective expense to the acid test. Is this outlay really needed to accomplish the goals I have for my company? Is it a vanity expense? Is this the best time to make this purchase? If I can't defer it, how can I do it more cheaply?

TAKEAWAY:
Your business budget needs to be at a survival level.

THOUGHTS TO CONSIDER:
1. Do you have any expenses that are not essential?
2. Is this purchase or expense something that can be delayed?

ACTION STEP:
Pretend that your initial funding has been cut by a third and revise your budget.

FOCUS ON NET PROFIT

I love former NFL coach Herman Edward's quote, "We play to win the game." That pretty much says it all. In business, we play to make a profit. To be more precise, we play to make a "net profit." In layman's terms, this is what you get to put in your pocket or the business gets to keep in its bank account, after all the bills are paid. Just because your business brought in a million dollars does not mean that you made anything.

You want to guard your net profit and keep this percentage as high as possible. Gross profit is what you bring in before expenses (Gross profit = sales - cost of goods sold). I would rather have a company that does $200,000 per year in gross profit but has a net profit of $100,000, because I only need one employee and may be able to work from my basement, than a high gross profit business with a net profit lower than $100,000.

Your net profit is the number you want to keep track of. This could be called your business "batting average." The easiest way to keep this number high is to keep your labor and fixed expenses low.

Here is the basic way to find out your batting average:
>Step 1: What are the total sales for your business?
>Step 2: Add all other revenues received to your total sales, and then subtract the amount of all of your business expenses. This is your net income.

TAKEAWAY:
Net profit is the critical number that matters.

THOUGHTS TO CONSIDER:
1. Always figure out ways to keep your net profit high.
2. Think like a baseball player. Your net income is your batting average.

ACTION STEP:
Be diligent about keeping expenses low and net profit high.

GUARD YOUR ACCOUNTS RECEIVABLE

Be a hawk with account receivables (money owed you). Establish, from day one, with any new account, when monies are due. "The sooner, the better" is my philosophy. When you buy groceries and gas, you pay at the time of purchase. That is how I expect to be paid. I do recognize sometimes this just is not possible. But I see too many business owners that have allowed customers to abuse their payment terms.

I cannot tell you how many business owners I know who are always stressed over money. It is because their accounts receivable are well overdue. They are afraid to pressure their customers to pay, thinking it will cost them business. If these are the customers you need to be in business, don't open your doors. But this problem can be avoided by having clear terms to avoid excuses, invoicing the day the project is completed, or for longer projects, invoicing on a regular schedule.

I strongly believe commercial accounts should not be given more than thirty days to pay. With regard to non-commercial accounts (home owners), they should always pay the day services are rendered. My experience has been that you can double whatever your terms are when customer's will actually pay.

Unfortunately, slow or late payment is a fact we all face. But each day you don't have that money is a day you lose investing in the growth of your business or another day you run on credit. "Many executives assume that the only way to boost collection is by hounding their customers more often. But they can save days in a lot of different ways," notes Les Kirschbaum, president of an accounts-receivable business. "You can often improve collection just by changing your terms and conditions of payment. So remember that you've got a range of options, all of which can have a positive impact."[59]

TAKEAWAY:
Guard your accounts receivable and tell your clients up front when money is due.

THOUGHTS TO CONSIDER:
1. How long can you allow your commercial customers to go without paying? Cut that number in half.
2. Can you see where having long overdue account receivables will put a stress on your cash flow?

ACTION STEP:
Create a protocol for when your accounts are due. Commit to guarding cash flow like you would your child around water.

[8]

LEARN FROM EXPERIENCE

The previous seven sections have taught you about many of the ins and outs of starting a successful business. You now have the tools you need to move forward with more confidence and a plan in place for success. The following lessons in this section offer some additional advice to help you avoid some of the mistakes I made and obstacles I found in my twenty years of starting and owning businesses. You don't have to make these same mistakes! Learn from others' mistakes, as well as successes, by reading through the advice in this section.

DON'T BECOME DEPENDENT

There are very few pieces of advice I can give you more valuable than this: Do not allow yourself to be too dependent on others. For instance, if you are not computer savvy, and all of your business reports and financial information are housed on a computer, then you are in trouble. If you don't have the passcodes to all computer accounts and voicemail systems, then you are not in control of your business.

I am passive in many of my businesses, but I have mechanisms in place that allow me to know what is going on at all times. Here are two ideas that worked for me to allow me to maintain control of my businesses without relying too much on others:

- In my service companies, I have a spiral-bound notebook with 52 pages, one for each week. An abbreviated view of customer contact information and money received is entered here before being logged in the computer. I can scan this book and know the call volume, how calls were generated, what was contracted for, and how much was received. This is like my car's dashboard instruments. I can easily tell if I am low on oil or need emergency servicing.
- I once owned a retail business where I received a text message every night at closing with sales for the day. I also had all business mail go to my personal office so I could be aware of the bills. If your staff knows you have no idea what's going on, you've lost control of your company.

To some degree, you are dependent on your employees, vendors, and contractors. The way you don't become *too* dependent is having a plan in place for when the unexpected happens. Susan Payton, a Marketing Communications Instructor, has a plan in place: "When an employee quits, it can be a shock, especially if you don't have a contingency plan to replace them. Become independent and prevent this by 1.) Having processes in place to make it easy to train a replacement and 2.) Insure you have enough employees to get the work done, rather than having extra strain on one person who will soon quit from the pressure."[60] Using the same logic, have alternate vendors you can depend upon when your regular vendor drops the ball.

TAKEAWAY:
You cannot allow yourself to be completely dependent on others.

THOUGHTS TO CONSIDER:
1. If one or two key people left the company, would your business still operate within 90% of its current effectiveness?
2. What information would you need to receive each day or week that would give you a dashboard reading of your company's current condition?

ACTION STEP:
Develop a dashboard system that allows you to know the state of your company within minutes.

HANDLE TERMINATIONS WITH CARE

The popular reality TV show; "The Apprentice" has made the phrase, "You're Fired" a popular slogan. The show concludes each week with billionaire businessman, Donald Trump, dismissing someone from the show with that phrase, followed by the individual quietly walking out of the boardroom. In real life, terminating someone's employment rarely ends with the person getting up, thanking you for the opportunity, and quietly walking out the door. In fact, it is sometimes unpleasant business, but it needn't always be.

I remember terminating a guy and offering to take some of the blame by saying, "I may not have described the extent of skills I needed in our initial interview." I was being kind to him. He went off in a defensive mode and let me know that I was "a piece of..." I let him go through his one-minute rant and off he went. My secretary overheard my conversation and asked me why I allowed the former employee to insult me. My response was, "There was nothing I could say to change the way he feels, and if anything, it will just drag out the conversation." I like King Solomon's words of advice, "Do not answer a fool according to his folly, lest you be like him."

I stand by what I said here, but there are also real-world reasons to keeping the conversation short and based on job performance. Apologies can make it look like you are uncertain of your decision. And finally, you may regret it. Anything you say can be held against you if the employee applies for unemployment, sues, or badmouths you to your other employees.

Other advice:

- Do not delegate the terminating of an employee to someone who does not have the skill or temperament to do this. If it is a high level termination, it may be wise to have someone in the room that can document why the person was terminated. It also can keep the situation from being confrontational.

- Know your state's employment laws in regards to termination. You can do an Internet search to obtain these laws by typing your state followed by the words "employment laws."

TAKEAWAY:
Keep the termination process quick, to the point, and do not defend yourself.

THOUGHTS TO CONSIDER:
1. Do you know your state's employment laws?
2. Do you plan to do the terminations at your business on your own? Are there people to whom you can delegate this task?

ACTION STEP:
Read your state's employment laws, especially as relates to termination, and create a termination process for your business.

THE CUSTOMER IS NOT ALWAYS RIGHT

I am going to let you in on two secrets: Customers are not always right, and you don't want every customer.

First, if the customer is right, then your employees are wrong. There are times when you need to draw a line in the sand, and supporting your employee will be more valuable than the customer. For instance, I've had a customer claim an employee did, said, or promised something that I believed was not true. I had known this employee for ten years and had never heard anything close to what this customer was saying. In this situation, I told the customer that I did not believe that my employee said or did what she claimed.

I do everything I can to not have to come out and say this directly. I use statements like, "Maybe the employee did not quite understand you." However, if pressed, I will say I do not think my employee did what the customer claims. The few times I had to do this, my employee and their co-workers appreciated that I stood up for them and they have since returned their loyalty. The fact is some employees are much harder to replace than some customers.

Second, sometimes you don't want the business of certain customers. For example, in one of my home service companies, we give free estimates, but I decided early on that we would not give free estimates to realtors. I did this because they are only getting figures to use in contract negotiations; they don't actually intend to use our services. After performing fifty or so estimates in our first two years in business and not getting one job from them, I changed our policy on giving everyone a free estimate.

I have numerous realtors say, "You do not want my business." I do not go for the bait. Instead, I simply say: "No, we're not a good fit for you." This might be hard to do if you need the business, but take this advice from the Washington Post's "On Small Business" blog: "You don't need to think of it as 'firing' your customers—you can reframe it as serving your top-quality customers and prospects better. That requires that you sometimes narrow your focus; the best companies don't try to be everything to everybody."[61]

TAKEAWAY:

The customer is not always right, and you do not want every customer.

THOUGHTS TO CONSIDER:

1. Can you see where the customer can be wrong?
2. Can you identify potential customers that are not a good fit for your business?

ACTION STEP:

Decide how you will handle customers that you know are wrong, before the situation actually arises.

DEALING WITH COMPLAINTS

Very few things can be more draining to a business owner than dealing with an upset customer. It is even worse when you know a mistake was made on your end. I try to delegate as much customer service as a business owner can get away with. However, there are times when I have no choice but to get involved.

My staff knows, even though I am busy, that they can always call me for support. This is especially the case when they feel unable to resolve a customer issue, or to resolve it professionally.

For years, I had little skill dealing with upset customers. For one thing, I do not like someone talking to me like I am either stupid or a child. We have all had customers do this. But I have learned a strategy that works nearly every time:

Ask the customer "Where did we mess up?" and "What could we do better in the future so this never happens to another customer?" Then I shut my mouth and let them talk, and I *never* interrupt. Allowing them to just talk without being interrupted is like a magic pill to an upset customer. If I say anything it is just to get them to talk further, like "Go on..." or "Really?"

Believe it or not, listening to an intelligent unsatisfied customer might help you to better run your business. Ron Kurtis learned this lesson as Total Quality Manager for the Air Force's Strategic Defense Initiative Programs: "Another benefit of dealing with complaints is that you can see weaknesses in your process or products that can be rectified. This will prevent possible future complaints or problems down the line. It is an effective form of customer feedback, although one you hope to eliminate."[62]

If you go into the conversation knowing that you want to keep this customer coming back, bending over backwards to resolve and amend the complaint should be easy. At the end of the conversation, I repeat what I heard them say. "I am sorry [whatever mistake we made] happened, and I am personally going to make sure we implement [what they said we could do better in the future]." I close by thanking the customer for his or her business and ask the person to trust us with more business in the future

TAKEAWAY:
Customer complaints, if handled properly, can be a valuable experience.

THOUGHTS TO CONSIDER:
1. Can you remember a time when someone handled a complaint from you with ease and skill, leaving you satisfied that you had been heard?
2. Do you have a tendency to interrupt?

ACTION STEP:
Teach the above method of handling complaints with your staff.

TRADES

Trading your product and/or service in the beginning is a creative and effective way to save initial start-up cash. Trading, or bartering, as it is also known, is an exchange for service or products instead of a traditional cash transaction. In fact, "$12 billion worth of goods and services are traded every year without any currency changing hands."[63] This arrangement can work well with accountants, bookkeepers, graphic designers, and countless other professionals that will provide services to you initially. I have to tell you, I am a big fan of trading; so let me give you a few secrets.

First, get a firm price for the services or product you are seeking to receive. I have found when candidates for trading know in advance that you are seeking a trade, they just add their fees to the trade, and you gain nothing in this transaction. So, never mention that you are seeking to trade up front. After receiving a quote you can call this person, (I have found it usually works best with small businesses or individuals who can make the decision), and offer your service/product as your form of payment.

Jim Blasingame, Google's 1# ranked small business expert stresses the value of bartering for the small business. "For example, with too much inventory and too little cash, barter can be part of a survival strategy in a bad economy. Slow-turning goods become the equivalent of cash to pay for something that in a better economy would have been covered by the cash flow and profits from customer sales."[64]

Do not be embarrassed to ask to barter. Trading has been around a lot longer than our present form of currency. I have used this method more times than I can count for service, retail, and direct mail companies I have owned. For instance, if you are opening a restaurant, I am sure the painter or accountant would not mind half their fee in food. It never hurts to ask!

Note: Bartering is a form of income, but you can deduct certain costs you go through in that barter. See the IRS page on bartering to keep things above board and take advantage of tax deductions.

TAKEAWAY:

Trading/bartering is an effective method of obtaining initial services you may need to start your business.

THOUGHTS TO CONSIDER:

1. Have you ever traded services before?
2. What professional services will you need initially?

ACTION STEP:

Consider trades as a method of funding services you're going to need.

JEALOUSLY GUARD YOUR TIME

Becoming a business owner is exciting, but it will bring with it new demands on your time. The number of people that will be trying to meet with you to sell you their services can be distracting. It will range from insurance, merchant services, to endless advertising, to name a few.

In the beginning, if you have never been the head of anything, this can seem fun because now you make all the decisions. But I caution you to guard your time, as it is a limited resource. People have come to expect immediate responses. Susan Payton advises, "Check your email a handful of times a day. Don't respond immediately if you don't need to. Your customers will learn your parameters of availability."[65]

If you have someone other than yourself answering the phone, never have that employee put a call directly through to you unless you know who is calling and you want to take the call. In short, never take the unexpected phone call. The person answering the phone should say that you are not available but ask what the call is in reference to.

If the caller fails to provide this information, your employee should say: "The owner does not return any calls without knowing specifically what it is in reference to." I have found this to eliminate 80% of un-wanted solicitations.

When a caller does reveal the nature of the call, and it appears to be a business solicitation, ask the caller to send an email summarizing what he or she is proposing. Reassure the caller that the company does review emails each day, and that if there's interest in discussing the proposal further, someone in the company will follow up promptly. This step will eliminate another 10% of unwanted solicitations.

One further tip: If you decide to set up a face-to-face meeting, make it for 15 minutes before the hour, such as 1:45pm. This secret has saved me hours of meeting time. When you meet on the hour (2pm) the person you're meeting thinks he or she has you for an hour. When you meet 15 minutes before the hour, they get the idea that it will be brief, so they come prepared.

TAKEAWAY:
Guard your time. You will have less of it once you start a business.

THOUGHTS TO CONSIDER:
1. If you will be answering the phone, politely tell callers you are very busy and ask that they email you information. If they say they will call back, say you will still be busy.
2. If you have someone else answering the phone, is there a process in place so that they never transfer phone calls to you unless you know what it is in reference to?

ACTION STEP:
Do not accept any drop-in meetings from those soliciting your time.

START OVER EVERY YEAR

Each year you need to set aside time to reflect and be deeply critical of your business. This is a time when you take out your business plan and review your previous mission, values, and goals. You ask yourself if you are staying true to those. You may need to change one of these declarations. I have had to alter mission statements over the years as my businesses evolved. As I get older, my values also change and need to be reflected in how I operate my businesses.

I would hope you have reviewed the goals of your company at least once per week during the first year of business, but if not, then this is the time. Ask yourself why you did not hit the ones your company fell short of. Were they realistic? Set new goals for the year ahead with a list of every action or event that is going to need to take place to reach them. Review your budget and income projections. These should be fine-tuned with all waste eliminated.

Picture what your business would look like if it were perfect in every possible way. How would it look and operate? This is a famed statement by business consultant, Brian Tracy. What would it cost to operate this perfect business and what would you need to change for it to reflect this picture? Next, knowing what your now know, what products and services should you continue to offer? Do not continue unprofitable activities just because they were in your original business plan. Be flexible and critical, only offering profitable products and services.

Finally, knowing what you now know about your staff and needs, whom would you re-hire? If you, after careful evaluation, would not re-hire someone, make the change fast and begin the next year with a better start.

TAKEAWAY:
Each year, have a time of critical analysis of your company.

THOUGHTS TO CONSIDER:
1. What products/services have not been as profitable as you thought they might be?
2. Which employees would you not re-hire knowing what you now know?

ACTION STEP:
Each year set aside at least one entire day alone to critically analyze your original business plan, current business, and staff.

DREAM BIG, THINK BIG

Be an optimist. What would you do if your business exceeds your expectations? I recently learned the story of Auntie Anne's Pretzels. In the beginning, the company was selling a variety of baked goods at fairs. However, the owner quickly realized that pretzels were the hot item, so she more than doubled their price and focused on selling these alone. It is now common to go to a mall and see an Auntie Anne's pretzel franchise. The company now sells more than $400 million in pretzels annually.

My own experience has taught me the same lesson. When I first started one of my businesses, my initial goal was to use the income to support my passions—playing golf and tennis. I projected $1,000 a week in sales, with $200 in net profit. This was a part-time business for me. But it wasn't long, though, before I began receiving over 50 phone calls per week. That was more than 10 times what I'd planned for. Millions of dollars, three divisions, and a beautiful office later, I had to enact a growth plan, and quick.

Dream big and plan big! Imagine your business succeeding beyond what you initially thought. Who would you hire if your business grew quickly? Should you expand into different locations? How would you put your hands on cash or credit if you needed to take advantage of your new growth? Do you have a model that should be franchised? Are you the right person to run this evolving company? The list of questions is endless, but the end goal is the same: prepare yourself for success.

"Impossible is just a big word thrown around by small men who find it easier to live in the world they've been given than to explore the power they have to change it. Impossible is not a fact. It's an opinion. Impossible is not a declaration. It's a dare. Impossible is potential. Impossible is temporary. Impossible is nothing."
-Muhammad Ali

TAKEAWAY:

Plan for success.

THOUGHTS TO CONSIDER:

1. How big of a market do you think you could serve with your current resource level?
2. Are you content to be small or do you dream of being larger? (There is no wrong answer!)

ACTION STEP:

Have a plan put aside if the business explodes with growth.

KEEP A START-UP JOURNAL

Throughout this book, I have encouraged you to ask yourself questions such as "why you are going into business?" In your business plan, I stressed the importance of having a mission, value, and vision statement. I also emphasized the need to set personal goals for your company. I suggested that you keep these statements and documents nearby as a source of constant encouragement and to remind yourself where you are going.

In the same way, it's important that you creatively visualize your "journey." One way to do that is to start keeping a journal. Fill it with ideas and inspirations for achieving success and prosperity. Start thinking of yourself today, right now, as a successful and prosperous entrepreneur. Affirm that every day.

Say, for example, you dream of your company being listed on the stock exchange. That's a terrific goal. Cut out an actual exchange listing and replace it with a mock listing for your own. Then glue or tape this "new" listing on a sheet of paper, and make a photocopy. It will look like your company is listed. Keep this in your journal or post it near your cash register.

If lack of income at your current job is your primary motivation for starting a business, put a copy of your pay stub in your journal. List the annual salary you want to make. If your main reason is to have more free time so that you can fish, get some promotional material from a fishing expedition you'd love to join.

Sound silly? It's not. Norman Vincent Peale once called it the "power of positive thinking." Nearly every book on achievement I've read has suggested that I write my goals down and find ways to visualize the things I want to own, be, or places I want to visit.

Shakti Gawain, who wrote the bestselling book Creative Visualization, once noted: "You create your opportunities by asking for them." Joe Vitale, author of The Attractor Factor, says: focus on images of prosperity, and prosperity will be yours.

It still takes hard work. Einstein once said: "Genius is 10% inspiration, 90% perspiration." However, it starts with inspiration. Be inspired every single day. Tell yourself in words and pictures what it is that you are meant to be.

TAKEAWAY:
Anticipate future success by creatively visualizing your steady progress toward it.

THOUGHTS TO CONSIDER:
1. Have you ever used a written goal or photo to motivate you?
2. Is there a quote that motivates you? Find a quote or two that motivates you and put it on the cover of your journal.

ACTION STEP:
Create a journal or "vision" book for your dreams and goals.

WANT TO LEARN MORE?

Are you looking for personal business start-up coaching?

Need help determining whether you or your business idea is a good fit for the entrepreneurial journey?

Do you have a passion for owning your own business?

VISIT US AT

www.8unbreakablerules.com

Suggested Resources

Books
10 Natural Laws of Successful Time and Life Management, By Hyrum W. Smith
Originally published in 1995

25 Ways to Win With People: How to Make Others Feel Like a Million Bucks, By John C. Maxwell
Originally published in 2005
http://www.johnmaxwell.com/

48 Days to the Work You Love, By Dan Miller
Revised edition in 2010
http://www.48days.com/

Goals!: How to Get Everything You Want- Faster Than You Ever Thought Possible, By Brian Tracy
Originally published in 2003

How to Win Friends and Influence People, By Dale Carnegie
Originally published in 1936

Rich Dad Poor Dad, By Robert Kiyosaki
Originally published in 2000
http://www.richdad.com/Home.aspx

So You Want to Start a Business: 8 Steps Before Making the Leap, By Edward D. Hess and Charles F. Goetz
Originally published in 2009

http://www.pearson.ch/Informatik/FTPrenticeHall/1449/9780137126675/So-You-Want-to-Start-a-Business-8-Steps.aspx

The 7 Habits of Highly Effective People, By Stephen R. Covey
Originally published in 1989
https://www.stephencovey.com/7habits/7habits.php

The Speed of Trust, By Stephen R. M. Covey
Originally published in 2006
http://speedoftrust.com/new/

Think and Grow Rich, By Napoleon Hill
Originally published in 1987

Duct Tape Marketing Revised & Updated: The World's Most Practical Small Business Marketing Guide, By John Jantsch
Revised and updated in 2011

Today Matters: 12 Daily Practices to Guarantee Tomorrow's Success, By John C. Maxwell
Originally published in 2005
http://www.johnmaxwell.com/

ORGANIZATIONS

Better Business Bureau
www.bbb.org
A nonprofit organization focused on advancing marketplace trust, consisting of 116 independently-incorporated local BBB organizations in the U.S. and Canada, coordinated under the Council of Better Business Bureaus (CBBB) in Washington, D.C.

National Federation of Independent Business (NFIB)

www.nfib.com

Founded in 1943, NFIB is the leading small business association representing small and independent businesses. Its mission is to promote and protect the right of its members to own, operate and grow their businesses

SCORE

www.score.org

Non-profit association providing free counseling and low-cost workshops to small businesses throughout the United States.

Small Business Association (SBA)

www.sba.gov

Since it's founding on July 30, 1953, the U.S. Small Business Administration has delivered millions of loans, loan guarantees, contracts, counseling sessions and other forms of assistance to small businesses.

Toastmasters

www.toastmasters.org

Toastmasters International is a non-profit educational organization that teaches public speaking and leadership skills through a worldwide network of meeting locations.

WEBSITES

Angie's List

www.angieslist.com

Angie's List is a website that aggregates verified consumer reviews of service companies as a way to "capture word-of-mouth wisdom". Angie's List has about 1.5 million subscribers throughout the United States and Canada who post an average of about 40,000 reviews each month.

Reputation.com

www.reputation.com

Reputation.com is a company based in California that offers online reputation management (ORM) and Internet privacy services. ORM is the practice of making people and businesses look their best on the Internet.

WORKS CITED

Abrams, R. (2012, November 16). *Small Business Strategies: Nurture your contacts.* Retrieved December 2, 2012, from USAToday.com: http://www.usatoday.com/story/money/columnist/abrams/2012/11/16/rhonda-abrams-entrepreneurs-contacts/1710077/

Abrams, R. (2012, December 9). *Strategies: How to handle that adrenaline.* Retrieved December 10, 2012, from USAToday.com: http://www.usatoday.com/story/money/columnist/abrams/2012/09/27/strategies-adrenaline-addiction/158094

Acohido, B. (2012, November 18). *Small firms benefit by outsourcing mundane tasks.* Retrieved December 10, 2012, from USAToday.com: http://www.usatoday.com/story/money/business/2012/11/18/efficient-small-business-back-office/1700265

Allison, S. (2012, April 10). *Startup Success: Throw Away Your Business Books.* Retrieved December 10, 2012, from Forbes.com: http://www.forbes.com/sites/scottallison/2012/04/10/startup-success-throw-away-your-business-books/

Applegate, J. (2001, October 29). *Hiring a Bookkeeper or an Accountant.* Retrieved December 22, 2012, from Entrepreneur.com: www.entrepreneur.com/article/45628#

Beesley, C. (2012, March 19). *5 Tips for Setting Your Salary as Business Owner.* Retrieved December 23, 2012, from SBA.gov: http://www.sba.gov/community/blogs/5-tips-setting-your-salary-business-owner

Berry, T. (2011). *Creating a Business You'll Love.* (M. Chimsky-Lustig, Ed.) South Portland, Maine: Sellers Publishing Inc.

Berry, T. (2010, September 21). *The Three Most Common Pricing Mistakes.* Retrieved December 25, 2012, from Bplans.com: http://timberry.bplans.com/2010/09/the-three-most-common-pricing-mistakes.html

Birnbaum, B. (n.d.). *Your Action Plan: Converting Your Strategy into Action.* Retrieved December 26, 2012, from BirnbaumAssociates.com: http://www.birnbaumassociates.com/action-planning.htm

BizFilings. (n.d.). *The Benefits of Incorporation.* Retrieved January 6, 2013, from BizFilings.com: http://www.bizfilings.com/learn/incorporation-benefits.aspx

Blank, S. (2012, December 4). *4 Types of Markets, 4 Ways to Gauge Them.* Retrieved December 21, 2012, from WSJ.com: http://blogs.wsj.com/accelerators/2012/12/04/4-types-of-markets-4-ways-to-guage-them/?KEY WORDS=business+model+simple

Blank, S. (2012, November 26). *Part I: Validate Your Business Model Start with a Business Model Not a Business Plan.* Retrieved December 10, 2012, from WSJ.com: http://blogs.wsj.com/accelerators/2012/11/26/start-with-a-business-model-not-a-business-plan/

Blasingame, J. (2011, August 15). *Is Barter Right For Your Small Business?* Retrieved December 26, 2012, from Forbes.com: http://www.forbes.com/sites/jimblasingame/2011/08/15/barter-for-small-business/

Bruder, J. (2012, May 25). *A Harvard Professor Analyzes Why Start-Ups Fail.* Retrieved December 12, 2012, from NYTimes.com: http://boss.blogs.nytimes.com/2012/05/25/a-harvard-professsor-analyzes-why-start-ups-fail/

Buschel, B. (2011, June 16). *Five Things I Wish I Had Known Before the Fire.* Retrieved December 23, 2012, from NYTimes.com: http://boss.blogs.nytimes.com/2011/06/16/ten-things-i-should-have-known-before-the-fire/

Christopher, J (2003). *When the Tripods Came.* Simon and Schuster, pp. vi.

Clapton, S. (n.d.). *6 Common Struggles of a Young Entrepreneur.* Retrieved January 1, 2012, from Under30CEO.com: http://under30ceo.com/6-common-struggles-of-a-young-entrepreneur/

Colao, J. (2012, November 12). *Can An Hour-Long Aptitude Test Predict Startup Home Runs? Adeo Ressi Thinks So.* Retrieved November 25, 2012, from Forbes.com: http://www.forbes.com/sites/jjcolao/2012/11/21/can-an-hour-long-aptitude-test-predict-startup-home-runs-adeo-ressi-thinks-so/

Copeland, M., & Malik, O. (2006, June). How to Build a Bulletproof Startup. *Business 2.0,* pp. 76-92.

Dewey, J. (1916). *Democracy and Education.*

NOTES

[1] Miller, 2012

[2] Edmunds,

[3] Strauss, 2012

[4] Allison, 2012

[5] Berry, Creating a Business You'll Love, 2011

[6] Zwilling, 2012

[7] Weitekamp, Levy, & Pruitt, 2012

[8] Clapton

[9] Oechsli, 2011

[10] Abrams, Strategies: How to handle that adrenaline, 2012

[11] Acohido, 2012

[12] Miller & Robinson, 2010

[13] Copeland & Malik, 2006

[14] Bruder, 2012

[15] James, 2012

[16] Jackson, 2011

[17] Tracy, 2012

[18] Blank, Part I: Validate Your Business Model Start with a Business Model Not a Business Plan, 2012

[19] Blank, 4 Types of Markets, 4 Ways to Gauge Them., 2012

[20] BusinessDictionary.com

[21] Strauss, 2012

[22] Christopher, 2003

[23] Berry, 2010

[24] Khosla, 2012

[25] Jackson, 2012

[26] Dewey, 1916

[27] The Startup Garage

[28] BizFilings

[29] Hanley, 2011

[30] Zwilling, 2012

[31] Logue, 2012

[32] Hughes, 2012

[33] Lloyd

[34] Lesonsky, 2012

[35] Lee, 1998

[36] Powell, 2012

[37] Applegate, 2001

[38] Mitchel, 2010

[39] Sellers, 2002

[40] Mooney

[41] Marcella

[42] Abrahms, 2012

[43] Entrepreneur

[44] DivisionX, 2012

[45] Quoted in Yu, 2012

[46] Quoted in McLoone, 2009

[47] National Business Research Institute

[48] Hines

[49] Overell, 2012

[50] Quoted in The Economist

[51] Abrams, 2012

[52] Hunter, 2012

[53] Feather

[54] Padnos, 2012

[55] Open: The Small Business Network

[56] Goltz, 2012

[57] Beesley, 2012

[58] Zwilling, Four Ways to Keep Burn Rates Low., 2011

[59] Quoted in Fraser, 2000

[60] Payton, 2012

[61] The Washington Post, 2012

[62] Kurtis, 2007

[63] Spitznagel, 2012

[64] Blasingame, 2011

[65] Payton, 2012

52344412R00130

Made in the USA
Middletown, DE
09 July 2019